W9-AGI-205

Dominion of
CANADA

with particular reference to Natural Resources

BAFFIN LAND

Hudson Bay

LABRADOR

FURS

FURS

PULPWOOD

TIMBER

NEWFOUNDLAND

ANTICOSTI I.

QUEBEC

St. Lawrence R.

Quebec

PRINCE EDWARD I

FARMING

NEW BRUNSWICK

Maritime Provinces

NOVA SCOTIA

Dartmouth

Halifax

ONTARIO

GOLD

ZINC

Montreal

NICKEL

PLATINUM

INDUSTRIAL AREA

Ottawa

L. SUPERIOR

L. MICHIGAN

L. HURON

L. ONTARIO

L. ERIE

Toronto

LOBSTERS and COD

Atlantic Ocean

CANADA : *America's Problem*

CANADA:
America's Problem

*

John MacCormac

THE VIKING PRESS * NEW YORK

1940

FIRST PUBLISHED IN JUNE 1940

SECOND PRINTING BEFORE PUBLICATION
THIRD PRINTING JUNE 1940

COPYRIGHT 1940 BY JOHN MAC CORMAC
PRINTED IN U.S.A. BY AMERICAN BOOK—STRATFORD PRESS, INC.
PUBLISHED ON THE SAME DAY IN THE DOMINION OF CANADA
BY THE MACMILLAN COMPANY OF CANADA LIMITED

TO MY FATHER

—Though He Will Disagree with Most of It

FOREWORD

The views expressed by the author of this book are in no sense those of the newspaper with which he is connected. They are strictly his own as a Canadian, and were published only after he had left the post to which they refer.

—JOHN MACCORMAC

CONTENTS

PART I

*

The Problem Stated

Canada Compromises American Isolation

CANADA makes isolation impossible for the United States. Canada makes neutrality a fiction. Any day while the present struggle lasts, the United States might be forced to choose between a war over Canada and abandonment of the Monroe Doctrine. The possibility is remote so long as Britain holds her own on land and controls the seas. But it is there.

Colonel Lindbergh's warning to Canadians in 1939 not to draw the United States into a war because they preferred a king to a president was tactless but not pointless. His statement at least served to direct public attention to the fact that Canada, for the United States, has become the most important foreign country in the world. The United States can affect neutrality toward other belligerents but geography makes it impossible for her to be neutral toward Canada. So does material interest, for there are more American visitors and more American dollars in Canada at any time than anywhere else outside the United States. But there are few countries about which Americans know less. American financiers have discovered it, American tourists have discovered it, but American editors have yet to discover it.

They know little about Canada because they have taken her for granted as a country half British, half American, and yet one-third French, lighted by the aurora borealis and the midnight sun, and populated chiefly by the Indians, the Royal Canadian Mounted Police, and the Dionne quintuplets. They have taken her for granted but now they must take her for better or worse. They must protect her at home while she wages war abroad.

This book is an attempt to indicate that the war will make Canada the air headquarters of the British Empire and its second line of defense strategically, industrially, and financially, a significant change of status which will alter her relations with Great Britain and still more vitally her relations with the United States. Particularly does it change the whole meaning of that American guarantee of Canada's territorial inviolability—the Monroe Doctrine.

Canada has long tacitly enjoyed the protection of the Monroe Doctrine although, unlike the other nations of the Americas which are so secured, she is part of a world system. That there is something anomalous about an empire of autonomous nations under a common king is not news. King George VI declared war on Germany on September 3, 1939, as King of England. For a week he was still formally at peace as King of Canada. During that time, by grace of a somewhat special interpretation of American neutrality regulations, he was able, as a peaceful neutral sovereign, to look on with approval while his Canadian ministers ordered and received airplanes from the United States. Here was a striking demonstration not only of the ambiguity of Canada's position as a nation wholly in and yet partly out of the British Empire but of another fact not generally recognized—that, thanks to geography and the Monroe Doctrine, Canada has infected the foreign relations of the United States with that ambiguity. She has forced the United States to combine the role of neutral with that of friend and protector of belligerent Canada.

This is a construction of his famous Doctrine which must make President Monroe turn in his grave. That a declaration originally designed to prevent the establishment in the Western Hemisphere of new European colonies or the re-establishment of old ones would ever be used to deny to Europe the right to strike back in any vital sense at an American country which might be striking vitally at Europe could not have occurred to him in his wildest dreams. Neither could it have occurred to Secretary Olney when, in connection with President Cleveland's invocation of the Monroe Doctrine in the boundary dispute between Britain and Venezuela in 1895, he declared that 3000 miles of ocean "make any permanent political union between a European and an American state unnatural and inexpedient." President Monroe did not foresee such complications flowing from his famous Doctrine because he believed with Secretary Olney that "The United States is practically sovereign on this continent and its fiat is law upon subjects to which it confines its interposition." Colonel Lindbergh evidently believes this too. But the United States, after a brief dalliance with imperialism, has become the most moral of nations. The policy first enunciated in 1794 in that Anglo-American agreement known as the Jay Treaty, "to promote a disposition favorable to friendship and good neighborhood," has been nailed to the masthead of the American ship of state by its present captain and there are no evidences that any considerable number of its crew would like to tear it down.

"Good neighborhood" did not inspire the Monroe Doctrine or its extension to Canada. The United States must prevent European conquest in the Western Hemisphere for her own security. But only a good neighbor would guarantee Canada against European aggression without forbidding her to throw stones at Europe. She would find it easier to do so, of course, if the windows that were being broken were those of her own potential enemy.

That is true in this war. It was true in the last. The Monroe Doctrine did not prove a complicating factor after 1914 because Britain controlled the seas, because sabotage was a better method than aggression against a country which was aiding Britain largely in the capacity of granary and recruiting office—you do not bomb wheatfields, and soldiers are most vulnerable when they are in troopships—and because America went to war herself. But Canada in this war is to be not only wheatfield and recruiting office but air base, factory, and bank. She is to train 15,000 Empire aviators every year that the war lasts, finding most of the money therefor. Mr. Anthony Eden, who announced the plan in the British Parliament, remarked that Canada's contribution might well decide the war, and there seems no reason to doubt him. The threat of German air power, as reported by Colonel Lindbergh, is said to have settled the issue at Munich. The use of Canadian air power in this war, opposed by Colonel Lindbergh, may decide it in Berlin.

Whether this is so or not, the first few months of this war have presented Canada in the role of the Empire's second center. The dream of those who have predicted she would become its heart seems less fantastic now. Westward the course of Empire takes its way. Historians, looking back, may one day discern the first sure sign of our changing times in the unique appearance of the British Crown in person in North America last summer. The experiment was a huge success. From coast to coast, south of the border as well as north of it, royalty played a gallant part before packed houses. When the show was over, it was evident, so far as Canada was concerned, that neither audience nor players would be quite the same again. King George found assurance and his voice. Queen Elizabeth discovered crowd appeal and that she had it. Canadians realized emotionally what they had learned formally in their history books, that they were heirs to the glamorous and glittering traditions of the British Empire. Royalty in a state coach might be an anachronism in the New World, but the subconscious thrives on anachronisms and it is the subconscious, the psychologists say, that governs. Not so much for what it caused as for what it revealed, the royal tour made evident what had been uncertain, that if Great Britain were dragged into war Canada would rally to her side.

Canada has rallied to her side but in a new role. Decentralization of the British Empire began when the colonies became dominions. Now it is in its second stage. Geography had long made it possible, strategy has now made it advisable, and German bombing may soon make it imperative.

Geographically, Canada's position, with one coast lashed by the Atlantic and the other laved by the Pacific, makes her a far more logical shipping center than the United

Kingdom. She has two transcontinental railroad systems and in the St. Lawrence a water route whose development will allow ocean-going freighters to make their way to the head of the Great Lakes, more than 1000 miles inland. Her transcontinental freight rates are framed to meet the competition of the Panama Canal so that they are in reality water rates. Britain's twenty best customers, in the order named, are the United States, Canada, Australia, India, Argentina, New Zealand, Germany, South Africa, France, Denmark, Netherlands, Eire, Russia, Sweden, Belgium, Malaya, Poland, Egypt, Nigeria, and China. Of the total trade she does with them, the United States, Canada, and Argentina account for 20 per cent, and 50 per cent of it is with countries that could be as well or better served, even in peacetime, from Canadian ports. In wartime they could be served infinitely better. From Vancouver to Brisbane is only 6780 miles, as compared with 11,700 from London to Brisbane. Halifax is less than 280 miles farther from Capetown than London is.

If Britain's long-term investments are considered, it is quickly obvious that their center of gravity is not in Europe. They totaled £3,726,000,000 at the beginning of 1931. Of this amount, £2,187,000,000, or 58.7 per cent, was with the British Empire. In all Europe, including Turkey, only £295,000,000, or 7.9 per cent, was invested. Canada accounted for 14.1 per cent, the United States for 5.4 per cent, Central and South America and Mexico for 22.4 per cent. So far as her investments are concerned, it would seem that Britain could almost afford to turn her back on Europe. India, however, introduces a complication. In India and Ceylon Britain has invested on long term £540,000,000, or 14.5 per cent of the total. India is not in Europe, but it might be argued that no power which did not dominate Europe could hold India. India, in fact, is the great difficulty which must be surmounted if the British Empire is to give way to the British Commonwealth of Nations. In India the British Empire still represents domination rather than co-operation. When they look at India Englishmen are reminded of Clive and Warren Hastings and the Koh-i-noor, but Canadians may be reminded of Amritsar and of a repressive aspect of British imperialism which has long been distasteful to them.

England has only coal and iron and a little pottery clay, and her coal mines are deepening. Canada has most of the natural essentials except cheap coal and she has the world's cheapest waterpower to replace that. She is next door to the world's principal supplier of cotton, and far nearer Australia's wool. She has food in abundance and room and to spare for the whole of England's population. This, in any event, is the age of electricity and alloys, of plastics and man-made fibers. England's industrial greatness was built on coal and iron, and that foundation is crumbling. You can read its future in the rusting machinery and the rusting men of her Black Country. The workers who make her fine wools could make them in Canada. The moist climate which helps her cotton manufacturers can be simulated by air conditioning after the pattern of Canada's own textile plants. If men and machinery could be transplanted en masse under Canadian rooftops they would find power cheaper and raw materials and food far more accessible even in peacetime and infinitely more so in time of war.

Strategically, shifting the Empire's center of gravity to Canada would make the Atlantic Ocean the new British Channel. In Britain industry is more vulnerable to air attack than anywhere else in the world. In Canada it cannot be bombed. England, as the headquarters of the Empire, represents too many eggs in one basket. England is too small, too thickly populated, too near her potential enemies, thus too vulnerable to attack. Her aircraft factories will be difficult to defend against intensive bombing. Her shipbuilding yards will be impossible to conceal and therefore exposed to even greater hazards. The torpedoing of the *Royal Oak* in Scapa Flow indicates that even as a naval base Britain's position is not what it was. These considerations have already led to Canada's selection as a new Empire air center and the basing of a substantial British fleet in Halifax Harbor. The Canadian Government's plan to build mine-sweepers, sub-chasers, and other minor naval craft in Canada and its expectation of orders for the construction of larger ones have been announced.

Canada is vast, scattered, protected by two oceans. Her coastline is immense but snow and ice and natural configuration defend it all save at a few points. More important immediately than these natural defenses is the paper protection of the Monroe Doctrine. In Canada, because of the Monroe Doctrine, the British Empire has a base which cannot become subject to serious enemy attack without drawing in the United States. The more important that base becomes, the more anomalous the position of its American protector. Germany's cry of "unfair" when President Roosevelt reaffirmed his guarantee of Canada after the outbreak of war is not likely to be her last word on the subject. She would not be silenced by a reminder that she herself has practiced every conceivable form of intervention in the affairs of other countries while ostensibly neutral. Still less would she be soothed by the argument that the United States is in a sufficiently ambiguous position without any help from Canada, since her contribution of the means of war to Britain and France may be as decisive as any aid the senior Dominion can render.

It may be as decisive but it is not likely to be more decisive. Without credits there are decided limits to the orders the Allies can place in the United States. But credits will be available in Canada and, as a consequence, Canadian industry will wax large on war contracts despite competition from the far more highly developed industry of the United States. In the last war the United States was supplying war credits and yet by 1917 Canada was furnishing half the shells used by the British armies in France and part of the requirements of Britain's allies as well. Now Britain cannot obtain American credits. Her purchases in the United States must be paid for in gold or in American dollars. But she can sell back to Canada the $2,700,000,000 of Canadian securities held by her citizens before she needs to ask for loans. She is already, in effect, beginning to use them to pay for her heavy imports from Canada. If she needs loans she will get them. To help finance her own contribution to the war, Canada is also ready to repatriate the $1,500,000,000 of American securities owned by Canadians, which have helped to offset the $4,000,000,000 odd which represents the investment of the United States in Canada. These figures add up to important money. Can-

ada, if the war lasts long enough, may become the chief
agency for mobilizing her own and United States resources
behind the Allied war effort. Montreal, which as a financial
capital has long wavered uncertainly between London and
New York, will probably emerge from the war with independent status. Like New York in the Great War, it will
have been prodded more or less reluctantly into the role
of world money center.

The war loans raised by the Canadian Government in
the Great War were its first domestic issues. Before the
Great War, Canada had obtained almost 90 per cent of her
capital requirements from Britain and the United States.
By the end of the war she was supplying more than 80 per
cent of them herself and she has continued to do so. By the
end of this struggle she will be helping to finance Great
Britain. When the Great War broke out Canada had no
central banking system. Now she has a government-owned
central bank and, under its aegis, a complete system of exchange control. She has also become the world's fourth
largest gold producer.

Two things seem likely to happen to Canada financially
as a result of this war. She will have financial greatness
thrust upon her. When hostilities cease she will not owe
Britain a cent and may be her creditor. She will have paid
off her debt to Britain with her exports and thus converted
it into an internal debt. It will be the war debt situation
again, but this time all in the family. To maintain the
value of her dollar she may have to repatriate the American securities her citizens hold. Although she cannot obtain credits in the United States, she can invite American
investment to help finance the war expansion of her indus-

try. That she will do so has already been indicated by the promise of her Foreign Exchange Control Board to grant American dollars for the remittance to the United States of profits on such investments. There seems to be nothing in United States neutrality regulations to prevent her re-selling to private American buyers the securities she repa-triates from Britain. That might mean that, in one way or another, she could mobilize some three billion American dollars for war purposes. The net result of all this will be to end British financial control over Canada and to in-crease her financial obligation to the United States, whose capitalists already own one-fourth of Canada's industry. The implications are interesting.

Any shift of the center of gravity of the British Empire away from Europe and toward Canada must be of extreme significance to the United States. An eagle may foster a lion cub. But when the cub grows up? To continue to throw a protecting wing of the Monroe Doctrine over a Canada with, say, 15,000,000 people, an industrial plant greater than Italy's, and one of the largest air forces in the world would be difficult unless the two parties concerned could agree always to pick the same side of the same quar-rels. Otherwise the United States might have to exercise a right to veto Canada's war ventures or fortify the famous 3000-mile border. Colonel Lindbergh and those who think as he does may have had the first course in mind. If they have been unable to commend it to the American public it is because spiritually the United States is in this fight on the same side as Canada. If the prewar policies of Britain and France have been criticized in the United States it has not been because they were too aggressive. Even more obvious has been the reluctance with which Canada again took up the sword she laid down twenty-one years ago. Perhaps even more than in 1914 Americans feel that if this is not their war it would be if they were Canadians.

It may be their war in the last analysis. When the terrifying potentialities of National Socialism were revealed in a recent book by the former Nazi chief of the Danzig Senate, Dr. Hermann Rauschning, it was disclosed that the spiritual author of the Nazi creed of world domination was General Professor Doctor Karl Haushofer, president of the German Academy at Munich. Dr. Haushofer, it was made plain, was the method in Hitler's madness, the brain directing the mailed fist of National Socialism, the inspiration behind the Nazi-Soviet pact which made the present war possible. Dr. Haushofer, then, must be accepted as an authority when he reveals the ultimate aim of Nazi policy. And Dr. Haushofer has defined it as the destruction, with the help of Russia, of "Anglo-Saxon world power," by which he means the United States and the British Empire. Europe is to be conquered and mobilized against the American continent. If that battle is won Germany will dominate the entire world. So writes the General Professor. There seems no reason to doubt that he means it.

The more intelligent advocate of isolationism will admit all this but argue that the "if" involved makes the percentage too small for American intervention to be worth while. He will agree readily that Anglo-French hegemony at its worst is preferable to the Nazi terror at its best. But, he will point out, there is no room for American soldiers in the Maginot line and America gives every other sort of help to the Allies by throwing open to them and them only her immense industrial resources. If she has found a way to do this while preserving a technical neutrality she has done all that could be expected of her. She has never made it her business to preserve the European balance of power. She has discovered from bitter experience that war is a poor way of safeguarding democracy. She is therefore justified, and well advised, in electing for isolation in this paradise of peace, the Western Hemisphere.

So runs the argument. It has only one flaw in it, a mere 3,700,000 square miles in extent, called Canada. Canada, so long as she fights in European wars and enjoys the protection of the Monroe Doctrine, makes isolation impossible for the United States. The Monroe Doctrine, when applied to a belligerent Canada, becomes a spearhead of aggression rather than a buckler for defense. It is transformed from a declaration of isolation into an entangling alliance. It links the United States with the British Empire, with Europe, and with European wars. It becomes, in short, the exact antithesis of what it was meant to be.

In making this clear, no disservice is done to Canada or to the winning of the war. Canada also has her isolationists but this book was not written by one of them. No one who lived next door to Nazidom in Vienna, listened nightly to the broadcast ravings of its professional maniac, and finally saw the brown flood seep through Austria's pathetic defenses to poison that ancient well of culture and infect a charming and childlike people with cruelty and unreason could doubt that it is a terror which threatens the whole world. British imperialism has been greedy and grasping at its worst. It has professed one thing and done another. But at least it has recognized, even if only by the care which it has taken to camouflage their circumvention, that there are standards of reason and justice. But Nazism denies both God and reason. It commands Germans to think with their blood. Rejecting simultaneously faith and science, it sets up its throne in the subconscious mind of man and asks its followers to deify the dark shapes that wander there. What National Socialism sought to make of Germany was a cunning madman, celebrating a Black Mass by the light of burning encyclopedias. Now the madman is running amok. Perhaps Britain and France, by better treatment of the patient, might have averted his mania. Certainly they could have prevented its spread. But in any event, when madness is abroad in the world, the duty of sane men is clear.

The problem which Canada represents for the United States is, therefore, not a vexed one in this war. In a sense Canada may render a psychological service to the United States by furnishing her with an opportunity to help the side she approves while staying on the sidelines herself. This was demonstrated by the loud chorus of disapproval that greeted Colonel Lindbergh's irritable admonition to the Canadians not to compromise American neutrality. The Colonel had obviously been too long away from home and had become out of touch with his own people. His outburst was predicated on a rather narrow logic, and made no allowance for racial sympathies. Even from the logical viewpoint there was, of course, an answer. If Canada compromises American neutrality vis-à-vis Great Britain, she compromises British neutrality vis-à-vis the United States. If she is an embarrassment she is also a hostage.

That is why, not only in this war but after it, American

discrimination in favor of Canada may bring a worth while harvest. A better-armed, more highly industrialized, and more thickly populated Dominion will undoubtedly emerge from the conflict if it lasts long enough, but so, in the nature of things, will an Americanization of her policies that will permit her to remain an acceptable neighbor and bedfellow under the blanket of the Monroe Doctrine. More important still will be an inevitable exercise of her influence in the British Empire to detach it from Europe and make it something with which the United States can cooperate with less suspicion that she may be used to further ends alien to her own views and interests.

It was intimated by semi-official spokesmen, though no firm offer was ever made, that part of the price Britain was prepared to pay to avert the present war was an arrangement for the common exploitation of colonies. It is now being intimated that a federated Europe and an open-door colonial policy may be the basis of peace. If that were so the British Empire might become less an empire and more a real commonwealth of nations. That is the kind of empire Canada would like. It would make it possible for her to remain British while steadily growing more North American. That is vitally necessary if she is to preserve her unity, which, under present conditions, has been maintained only by escape mechanisms that have left her with a steadily developing case of schizophrenia.

Of more interest to Americans is that the greater Canada's influence in the British Empire, the greater the influence of the United States. If she stays in the Empire Canada's care must be to assure that America and Britain walk hand in hand and preferably down the paths of peace. She must exalt her traditional role of interpreter of the two Anglo-Saxon great powers to that of co-ordinator. She will not do this out of pure love for the United States nor even because she fears that the views of Colonel Lindbergh may some day be shared by the State Department. She will do it for the sake of domestic harmony, which is seriously threatened by all wars in which she engages but more particularly by those in which the United States does not. It is only a few years since the erstwhile French Nationalist leader, Mr. Henri Bourassa, boldly declared in the Canadian House of Commons that as between Great Britain for war and the United States for peace, Canada must decide for the United States. And when Mr. Bourassa said that, he was no longer a fiery Nationalist but a snowy-haired elder statesman.

While Canada remains British she makes complete isolation impossible for the United States. But if Canada's effect on the United States is to draw the United States into European affairs, her effect on England is to detach England from them.

The process of retreat to Canada, carried out to its logical conclusion, would leave Britain a cultural and strategic rather than an industrial and commercial outpost. She would have a far better-balanced economy. Her population would be large enough to serve as garrison, but small enough to grow part of its food, store more of it, and be supplied, even in the face of a submarine blockade, with the rest.

It is difficult to imagine the present occupant of 10 Downing Street as contemplating such a future for his country with equanimity, far less contributing to its realization. But there are Englishmen who would welcome it.

One of them wrote a book about it in which he estimated the optimum population of Britain at 19,000,000 and chose Canada as a new home for the surplus 26,000,000.[1] His reasons were that Canada was "the nearest of the great un-peopled dominions, where there could never be any short-age of space, food, amusement, waterpower, minerals, tim-ber, or employment," where "we should possess all the necessary materials for peace or war," and where "we should be putting ourselves right beside the United States, which have the same interests in preserving peace as ourselves." Four years ago, Mr. Osbert Sitwell urged a similar mass-migration of his countrymen across the Atlantic and rein-forced his argument with a reminder that the Emperor Constantine had saved Roman civilization from destruc-tion at the hands of barbarian enemies for another thou-sand years when he removed his capital to Byzantium. Lord Beaverbrook has been advocating in London for many years that the English should concentrate on their own Empire and join the Americans in isolation from Europe.

The postwar alternatives for that troublous continent seem to be either a United States of Europe or a Russo-German hegemony. The latter would make withdrawal to Canada imperative. The former is now being discussed in the United Kingdom. But between the lines the disillu-sioned inhabitant of these Americas may fancy he discerns a firm intention to set up no federal union that would not be the "balance of power" in another guise. "The balance of power," wrote Johannes Stoye, discussing the British Empire from the "geo-political" viewpoint adopted by

[1] *The Next British Empire,* by R. A. Piddington.

Stoye's countryman General Haushofer as the basis of Nazi expansionist ideas, "has ended by becoming purposeless. The idea today is to keep out of war, for war in an age of airplanes, long-range guns, and submarines means destruction for both victor and vanquished."

But the only substitute for the balance of power, if Britain is to continue to base herself on Europe, is collective security and Britain deserted that when she refused to help the League of Nations stop Japanese aggression in Manchuria and Italian conquest of Ethiopia. So, even though this famous equilibrist performance has cost England dear and Europe dearer—as witness the present balance of power between the Siegfried and Maginot lines—England can scarcely change her act while she holds so many of the Empire's golden eggs in her small basket. But a British Empire securely based on the other side of the Atlantic could forswear vaudevillian for more legitimate roles.

There are Englishmen who have foreseen the necessity. Among them is the eminent British historian, Professor Arnold Toynbee, who, envisaging such a world struggle as may now be in the shaping in Europe, said he believed "that the victory in that awful struggle will go, not to those powers [who provoked it] but some Great Power that combines a continental structure with a command of modern technique and with democratic institutions to give its people staying power. This combination of winning points is only to be found in English-speaking North America, by which I mean the United States reinforced by the English-speaking parts of Canada."

As things are, Britain is fighting a losing fight even if

she is winning this war. Nothing but an overwhelming defeat could be more embarrassing to her than a shattering
victory. She would not know what to do with the pieces.
An atomized Europe might end Hitler, but it would not
stop Stalin. A strong Germany under conservative leadership might stop Stalin but could not long be denied hegemony over Europe.

The alternatives to a victory are defeat or stalemate followed by a negotiated peace. Defeat would mean not retreat but a disorganized flight across the Atlantic. A negotiated peace in Europe that could be anything but an
uneasy peace defies the present wit of man to conceive. An
uneasy peace after a long war in which industry and civil-
ian populations had suffered from intensive air attack and
were faced with a quarter-century of crushing taxation to
pay for it would probably convince the average Englishman that he had had about enough of it. Knowing a better
'ole, he would go to it. He alone of Europeans has the
chance.

Of late years Britain has seemed to tire of the burden of
world leadership and to appear not only willing but eager
to shift it to the United States. The duty might be divided.
The more closely British and American policies approxi-
mate each other the easier to merge the Pax Britannica
into a Pax Americana. Canada would welcome it. In so far
as she waxed important as the second center of the British
Empire she would and could contribute to it. She would
become an asset on the balance sheet of the Monroe Doctrine, whereas now she is a liability.

An English-speaking Union may be a consummation far

less remote than once appeared. Hitler has set a fashion which other races, for their own protection, are almost compelled to follow. Was it not his great countryman Bismarck who said that the greatest political fact of modern times was "the inherited and permanent fact that North America speaks English"? There is an Anglo-American community of ideas and interests which not even unpaid war debts and a repudiated League of Nations have been able to dissolve. There is an English-speaking Union now, and its charter is contained in the carefully framed Neutrality Laws of the United States. Perhaps it would be better if it never existed in name. A strong Canada which was at once a constituent of the British Empire and a member of the Pan-American Union might serve the same ends and excite fewer resentments.

It would undeniably solve many of Canada's difficulties. In its present state Canada is the problem child of the Western Hemisphere. It is a typical product of family estrangement. Canada has an Oedipus complex which, in her relations with the mother country, prevents her ever growing up. Afraid to join the Pan-American Union for fear of compromising her position in the British family of nations, Canada has hesitated to lift her voice in that family council for fear of being committed to its decisions. "Canada," exploded one of her resentful intellectuals recently, "is in international affairs not a man but a woman! 'Whither thou goest,' she says to her father, John Bull, 'I will go.' "

And now she has gone into a war. That it is a just war does not alter the fact that she never lifted a voice while it was in the making either to approve or to condemn it, and her appointment on the battlefield, technically made by herself, was actually foreordained by factors beyond her control. How and why this is so is something Canadians scarcely understand. Americans cannot be expected to comprehend it, but an effort will be made to explain it in succeeding chapters.

2

What Will America Do about Canada?

THE MONROE DOCTRINE has proved elastic enough to permit Canada freedom to go to war without sacrificing its advantages. Like the debutante's girdle, it has provided local support without interfering with long-range activity. Even if Canada emerged from this war with a more important and matronly figure, the Doctrine could probably be stretched to cover it—if the maker were willing. If not, it might turn suddenly into a straitjacket. Whether that willingness can be expected is the theme of this chapter.

To ascertain what the United States would do in situations that are still completely hypothetical is obviously impossible. But a basis for speculation may be established by reviewing former American attitudes and testing the present temper of public opinion.

That Canada has become the principal beneficiary of the Monroe Doctrine perhaps proves that history has a sense of the fitness of things, since that famous declaration had its origin in British, not American sources. In 1823 George Canning, British Foreign Secretary, suggested to Richard Rush, American Minister in London, that a joint declaration be made by Britain and the United States to meet the situation caused by Spain's loss of her South American colonies and the ambitions of France. What he had in mind was a declaration that Spain could not hope to regain her colonies, that neither Britain nor the United States desired them, but that they could not with indifference see them transferred to any other power. "I resolved," boasted Canning later, "that if France had Spain it should not be Spain with the Indies. I called the new world into existence to redress the balance of the old."

Like many another bright idea, Canning's suggestion was to bear unexpected fruit. He might not have been so proud of it seventy-two years later, when it was used against Britain in the Venezuelan boundary dispute. As it was, President Monroe consulted Jefferson and Madison. They favored acceptance of the British proposal in some form. But John Quincy Adams, Secretary of State, was against a joint declaration and Jefferson cautioned that "our first and fundamental maxim should be never to entangle ourselves in the broils of Europe; our second, never to suffer Europe to intermeddle in cis-Atlantic affairs." The President finally decided to make a declaration on the sole responsibility of the United States.

Two paragraphs in the President's message to Congress set the Doctrine forth. He declared that "the American continents, by the free and independent condition which they have assumed and maintained, are henceforth not to be considered as subjects for future colonization by European powers." But as time went on, its application was widely extended. Probably the most ambitious claim based on it was Secretary Olney's famous declaration quoted in the first chapter of this book. The most authoritative recent official analysis of it may have been the memorandum submitted to President Woodrow Wilson in 1914 by Robert Lansing, then counselor for the State Department but shortly afterwards Secretary of State.

"The Monroe Doctrine," wrote Mr. Lansing, "is in substance that the United States considers the extension of political control by a European power over any territory in this Hemisphere, not already occupied by it, to be a menace to the national safety of the United States. In 1823, when the Doctrine was enunciated, the dangers of the extension of European political power on this continent lay in the possible occupation of unsettled regions and in the conquest of the territory of an independent American state. Later, during the Polk Administration, another danger was recognized in the possibility of a voluntary cession of territory by an American state to a European power and the Monroe Doctrine was shown to be broad enough to include this means of acquiring political dominion. The inclusion of voluntary cession among the acts of acquisition against which the Monroe Doctrine is directed introduces the necessary corollary that it may be invoked against an American government as well as against a European government.

"It is manifest from this that the Monroe Doctrine is a national policy of the United States and also that it is not a Pan-American policy. The opposition to European control over American territory is not primarily to preserve the integrity of any American state—that may be a result but not a purpose of the Doctrine. The essential idea is to prevent a condition which would menace the national inter-

ests of the United States. The Monroe Doctrine is founded
. . . upon the superior power of the United States to com-
pel submission to its will whenever a condition arises involving European control over American territory, which,
because of the permanent nature of the control, is considered to be a menace to the national safety of the United
States. . . . In its advocacy of the Monroe Doctrine the
United States considers its own interests. The integrity of
other American nations is an incident, not an end. While
this may seem based on selfishness alone, the author of the
Doctrine had no higher or more generous motive in its
declaration. To assert for it a nobler purpose is to proclaim a new Doctrine."

There is no substantial difference between Mr. Lansing's
interpretation of the Monroe Doctrine and that of Secretary Olney eighteen years earlier. Both are an assertion of
American hegemony in the Western Hemisphere. During
President Roosevelt's regime of good neighborliness an
effort has been made to take the sting out of the Doctrine
so far as it applies to the other nations of this hemisphere
but to widen its application against Europe. The United
States endeavored to assure its neighbors that co-operation,
not coercion, was the keynote of the Doctrine. With their
co-operation it has lately attempted to make an American
preserve, not only of the land mass of the twin continents
but of the waters of the sea for an average distance of 300
miles from their coasts. At the time of writing the attempt
had not succeeded and the claim had been rejected by
England, France, and Germany.

Germany's reason included the argument that "by making an exception from the Monroe Doctrine in favor of

Great Britain and France the neutral American governments have at the outset fundamentally and seriously endangered the success of the zone of security proposed by them. The discrimination thus made between the position of Germany and her opponents might perhaps be removed to a certain extent if Great Britain and France would pledge themselves, under guarantee given by the American states, not to employ the above-mentioned possessions and islands [British and French possessions in the Western Hemisphere] as primary or supporting bases for acts of war. Even if they should do so, the fact remains not only that the territory of the belligerent state, Canada, adjoins the above-mentioned zone in the West and in the East, but also that parts of the Canadian territory are actually encircled by the zone."

Germany has thus twice taken occasion to rub in the fact that Canada makes isolation impossible for the Western Hemisphere and the United States. The United States has perceived this from early Revolutionary days and only in recent years has reconciled herself to it. For 135 years she tolerated Canada only as an apple is tolerated while it is ripening on the tree. She tried to include Canada in the Revolution. When Jefferson heard that General Montgomery had occupied Montreal he wrote to John Randolph that "in a short time we have reason to hope the delegates of Canada will join us in Congress and complete the American Union."

Hopes of annexation were not dissipated by the Treaty of Paris. The extinction of British rule on the American continent by the conquest of Canada was at least one of the objects of the war of 1812. It was felt that otherwise the United States could never be completely secure. Jefferson declared in 1812 that without the cession of Canada peace would be impossible. Representative Nathaniel Macon of North Carolina asserted that Canada was absolutely necessary to the peace and happiness of the nation and Thomas Bolling Robertson of Louisiana said that the power of Britain must be extinguished in America. The war of 1812 failed to accomplish its purpose but the purpose was not relinquished. Madison wrote to President Monroe in 1818 that Canada in British hands would be a constant source of dispute which both Britain and the United States should be equally anxious to remove. In 1823, the year the Monroe Doctrine was enunciated, Madison suggested to Richard Rush, American minister in London, that he appeal to the British Government to cede Canada as a measure which would make for permanent peace.

Both in Canada and in Great Britain, the Canadian rebellion of 1837 was attributed by the authorities to American inspiration. This charge was unfair so far as the American Government was concerned, although it was true that border Americans enlisted in the insurgent movement. The son of General Van Rensselaer of Albany became military commander of the forces of William Lyon Mackenzie, who led the rebel movement in Upper Canada, and raised a thousand men.

After the American Civil War annexationist ideas were strengthened. The reciprocity treaty of 1854 was dropped in the expectation that it would force Canada, for want of markets, to join the United States. In 1866 Chairman Banks of the Committee on Foreign Affairs reported a resolution suggesting that when the State Department was informed that Britain and the Canadian colonies accepted annexation the President should proclaim that Nova Scotia, New Brunswick, Lower Canada, Upper Canada, and the territories of Selkirk, Saskatchewan, and Columbia should be admitted to the United States as states and territories. Some members of Congress thought that annexation could best be achieved by giving the Fenians free rein. A bill to modify United States neutrality laws of that time to permit military expeditions against friendly powers passed the House of Representatives unanimously but was lost in the Senate. Actually, the Fenian raids on Canada helped to bring about, not annexation, but the confederation of the Canadian colonies into the Dominion of Canada in 1867. It caused deep annoyance in the United States. The House of Representatives unanimously approved a resolution from the committee on foreign affairs expressing the solicitude of the American people concerning the confederation of the Canadian provinces without the consent of their people and hazarding the prediction that the effect would be to increase the embarrassment already existing between Great Britain and the United States.

It was partly to offset confederation that the United States bought Alaska from Russia. Secretary Seward admitted in an interview that the purchase was intended to prevent the extension of the British coastline on the Pacific and to hasten the day when Canada would form a political union with the United States that would enable it to develop its resources and would remove a leading source of friction between England and the United States. Senator Sumner declared that the treaty with Russia was "a

visible step in the occupation of the whole North American continent." The United States was simultaneously negotiating for purchase of the Danish West Indies, and the
acquisition of Greenland had also been recommended as a
further step toward outflanking Britain's Canadian colonies. The purchase of the Danish West Indies, now the
Virgin Islands, was actually consummated in 1917 after
the Danish minister had been plainly informed that in
certain circumstances, such as the absorption of Denmark
by a European great power, the United States might feel
compelled to occupy them anyway. As a *quid pro quo* the
United States promised not to object to an extension of
Danish occupation of Greenland.

Between 1869 and 1871 three separate suggestions were
made to the British Government by that of the United
States that Canada should be ceded, partly to meet the
claims against Great Britain arising from the depredations
of British-built Confederate commerce raiders during the
Civil War and partly to remove a source of danger to good
Anglo-American relations. Sir Edward Thornton, British
minister in Washington, replied that Britain did not wish
to keep Canada but could not part with it without the
consent of the Canadians. President Grant in an annual
message to Congress, anticipating the "not far distant" ter-
mination of European political connection with the American continent, suggested that the necessary annexations
might include "perhaps Canada if she is amiable or if she
is troublesome and ungracious."

Much was heard of annexation toward the close of the
Cleveland administration. The views of the succeeding
Harrison administration were reflected by a confidential

memorandum in the State Department declaring that the essential task for American statesmanship was to "unite the continent, secure its independence, and prevent the northern part of it being turned into an outpost of European reaction antagonistic in spirit and institutions to the rest." It was argued that this would exclude war from the American continent. Annexation by coercion, it was recognized, would be unwise but it was suggested that Britain would not object to ceding possessions which had been the source of so many liabilities and disputes.

In 1895 came the Venezuelan boundary dispute and Secretary Olney's declaration that any permanent encampment on American soil by Europe was unnatural and inexpedient. Until the defeat of reciprocity in Canada in 1911 Americans continued to think that the annexation of the Dominion was not only expedient but inevitable, and revealed it somewhat too plainly in the speeches of President Taft and Champ Clark recommending the reciprocity treaty. Until 1921 American legislators still thought of Canada as a British possession to be bartered away by Britain if necessary. When in that year a bill was introduced in Congress for construction of the St. Lawrence ship canal three counter-measures were proposed, two of which involved the cession of Canadian territory in payment of Britain's war debts. Even in 1923 the Senate insisted on attaching a rider to the Halibut Fisheries Treaty with Canada which indicated that she was still considered a British possession.

It took a long time to realize that Canada not only did not want to be annexed by the United States, but was asserting an autonomy of her own as against Great Britain.

Americans had thrown a king overboard. The fact that Canada refused to jettison monarchical institutions and the British forms of government deceived them—it even deceived eminent American historians—into believing that Canadians had not yet attained freedom.

For nearly a generation nothing has been heard from any responsible American statesman on the subject of annexation. Americans have realized that Canada is not a danger to them as a possible base for attack. It is recognized that this country, which can defend itself so easily against assault from overseas, is helpless in the face of aggression from land. Colonized Canada is a narrow band nowhere farther than 200 miles from the American frontier. Its communications could be cut, its spine could be broken, its cities could be bombed. The two countries are so closely connected that such an attack would seem almost worse than civil war. If Canadian cities were bombed, a substantial part of the wealth that would be destroyed would be lost by American investors. If Canada were annexed there would be an uproar from American farmers, who would find themselves unable to compete, and since more than 1000 American firms already have branch plants in Canada, there would be no particular rejoicing among American manufacturers.

For these reasons, and because Americans are a friendly and generous if violent people, with no long memory for old hates and none of that half-mad, half-mystical sense of racial mission that troubles the Germans, they have learned to ignore the Canadian border rather than to resent it. Certainly nothing could be more generous than America's treatment of Canada in this war. If her neutrality regulations had been drafted by Canadians, they could scarcely have been more accommodating. Canada can buy warplanes in the United States. Germany cannot because they must be pushed or towed, not flown, across the American border. The ports of St. John and Yarmouth have been excepted from the belligerent zone which American ships may not enter. This has made it possible for American oil to be brought north by sea, both for Canadian consumption and for transfer to British ships which then proceed in convoy across the Atlantic. It has made it possible for Canada to trade in American ships with countries outside the belligerent zone. In other ways that it must remain for history to disclose, the American authorities have accommodated themselves to the sometimes difficult situations created by Canada's belligerency.

That is the situation now. The question is what it will be when the war is over and whether new circumstances may then exist which will alter the views of Americans. It is a subject on which official enlightenment cannot be expected. But the official mind, when it can be induced to speculate, seems to envisage three possible situations.

One of them would be produced by the decisive defeat of England and France. That would almost automatically result in Canada's independence under American auspices while the smaller possessions of Britain and France in this hemisphere, whose transfer to the victors might also come in question, would either be allowed to assert a qualified autonomy or be taken over by the United States for strategic purposes. Unlike the rest of the British Empire, Canada would be in no danger of falling prey to Germany or Russia unless the American fleet were destroyed. She would lose much of her importance in world affairs and fall irrevocably into America's orbit. But she would be safe while the United States was safe.

The second situation envisaged is that which would be produced should Britain emerge from a long, exhausting, and indecisive war, not defeated but so weakened that she must decline to the status of a second-rate power. In such circumstances Canada might assume a larger importance in the British Empire but the Empire would have less importance in the world. She would no longer be able to dictate to Europe. Her crown colonies, as part of the price of peace, might be thrown open for general exploitation. The Empire would be replaced by the Commonwealth. In such a situation Canadian-American relations would remain on their present basis.

The third possibility is that Britain and France may win decisively but that Britain, as a result of war experience, may elect to base her Empire in the Western Hemisphere. Leaving the United Kingdom as a garrisoned outpost to command Europe's sea exits and entrances, she pursues her imperial designs from Canada and, thus securely seated, continues to insert a long finger in all the world's pies. It is freely admitted in Washington that this would create a new problem in Canadian-American relations. Only if British and American policies were closely co-ordinated would the American public, it is thought, view such a situation without alarm. Such close co-ordination must involve agreement between the English-speaking peoples about the sort of world they wanted and the methods which could be used to achieve it. Canada, it is admitted, could play the principal role in effecting such an integration if it were possible at all. She could never hope to rival the United States, either in resources or population, so that the wealthier and stronger she grew, the more important she would become as a hostage, the more convincing as a pledge of friendly behavior, the more influential in Empire councils.

But though this theoretical possibility is admitted there seems to be little informed belief in Washington that this is how matters will develop. Rather, Canada is seen to be pursuing a course that will sooner or later detach her from Great Britain. In this, official opinion seems to agree with the view lately expressed by Mr. Lionel Curtis, that close student of the British Empire, that Canada must be left out of future imperial calculations.

Meanwhile, Americans, far from disapproving, seemed pleased—one could say almost proud—when Canada threw in her lot with Britain in this war. This feeling exists strangely side by side with the passionately reiterated determination to stay aloof from it themselves and a disposition to resent the British blockade and censorship as their impact is felt by the United States. This paradoxical parallelism of opposed ideas indicates how remarkably Canada, regarded for a century by Americans as the chief troubler of their relations with Great Britain, has changed her role. It also demonstrates how enduring is the damage done to British prestige in America by the course pursued by the Baldwin and Chamberlain governments. If there was a nation more execrated in the United States than Fascist Germany it was Bolshevist Russia. They have been twin devils in the American demonology, and they have done nothing of late to redeem themselves. But the fact that they are hated has

failed to make their Allied enemies liked. Perhaps too
many chronicles of cruelty and terror have blunted the
moral world-sense of the American people, perhaps it is a
defense mechanism against being drawn in, but there is a
growing tendency to consider this skeptically as merely another in the long succession of European wars. The last such
struggle was called the World War; this one is significantly
termed, in American references, the European war, although it is no more European than the last one.

A corollary of this attitude is that the United States is
taking steps to defend the isolation into which she has
withdrawn. In an election year otherwise remarkable for
economy in public spending, her fleet is being greatly en-
larged, the ideal now being a navy big enough to protect
both coasts without the assistance of the British fleet; there
are larger military appropriations and new provisions for
the defense, with the help of neighboring Latin-American
nations, of the Panama Canal. Already isolation is costing
dear, but there is no sign that Americans are not ready to
pay for it.

In other circumstances, Canada might represent a psychological danger to this isolation. If it were a more spectacular war and Canada's soldiers had already been called
upon to play the same illustrious role in it that they played
in the early days of the last one, it would be more difficult
for Americans to dismiss it as something unhappy but far
off, the flaring up of an incurable disease endemic in Europe rather than democracy's stand against the brown terror and the red. Already there has been a dribble of young
Americans into Canada's forces. When and if Germany
attacks in full force and Canada's air scheme begins to play

its expected part, the dribble may become a flood and America's determination to stay neutral may be more severely tested.

If the Allies manage to win this war by their own unaided efforts or hold their own long enough to effect some sort of compromise peace, it seems improbable that the United States will intervene. Certainly no argument that she "should" get into this war is called for or likely to prevail in the present mood of the country. But if the Allies begin to lose the war, a totally new situation will be created. Intervention will cease to be a merely moral issue and will have to be considered, pro and con, on the basis of sheer self-interest. Can the United States afford to let Germany and Russia dominate the Old World?

Faced by the Italian conquest of Ethiopia and the imposition by Germany and Italy of a Fascist regime on Spain, England and France betrayed rather than championed the democratic principle. Old World democracy stultified itself by making terms with Fascism; Fascism by allying itself with Communism; Communism by allying itself with Fascism. No sincere believer in any of these three systems could regard this war as anything but a choice of evils. But—however inadequate as judged by recent performances—in this struggle Britain and France are still the only representatives of individualism, capitalist democracy, and world free trade. If they are beaten, these principles will be replaced in Europe, Asia, and Africa by totalitarianism and the sort of economic nationalism which, with the aid of barter agreements, quickly metamorphoses into a new kind of economic imperialism.

Individualism, capitalist democracy, and free commerce

are the three dimensions of the world the United States has lived and prospered in. They are almost what "Americanism" means. The United States has heavy material as well as political investments in such a world. What if she has granted no war credits to the Allies? She owns almost one and a half billion dollars' worth of British and French securities as compared with half a billion dollars' worth of German securities. If Britain and France lose the war it may be taken that their securities will become about as collectible as the German ones. The United States has $18,-000,000,000 of gold, almost three-quarters of the world's total monetary supply. If Germany wins the war, gold will cease to be a medium of international exchange, for the Germans, who have had to finance their war preparations without it, will certainly see no reason to buy it with their goods after the war nor allow the Europe they will control to do so. Gold-dominated international finance is one of the things Germany says she is fighting against. In a world dominated by Germany America's eighteen billion dollars of gold might not be worth much more than its weight in iron.

A minor point is that Great Britain is also the best customer of the United States. But if she lost her empire and fell under the heavy yoke of Germany, her purchases must decline. Germany, which has achieved at heavy cost a substantial measure of autarchy within her own narrow borders, would find it much easier to impose on Europe and why should she not do so? She would have the British colonies to draw on, with the possible exception of Oceania, to which Japan might insist on helping herself with the Netherland Indies for good measure.

If the United States allowed the Allied cause to fail, Canada would immediately present a vital issue. It is impossible to escape the conclusion that Britain, seeing herself on the road to complete defeat, would transfer as much of her resources and population as she could to her senior Dominion, where they could enjoy the protection of the Atlantic Ocean and the Monroe Doctrine. She would probably seek to transfer a substantial portion of her merchant marine to Canadian registry and perhaps even part of her navy. Neither is it likely that Australians and New Zealanders would stay long in Oceania if Japan took it over.

What would the United States do in such a situation? Would she close the frontiers of this continent to a new flood of refugees, this time of her own blood and language? One can hardly imagine Americans refusing a New World sanctuary to fugitives from the cradle of their own race. It would also be to the interest of the United States, faced with the necessity of defending Canada, to see it as populous and productive as possible. It would equally be in the interest of Germany to see that its victims and its booty did not escape to found overseas a new nucleus from which the persistent British race might again sally forth in years to come. Almost inevitably, Canada would furnish a cause of war in such conditions unless Germany found herself too weakened in the hour of her triumph to take on a new and powerful antagonist. She would undoubtedly regard such a development with the virtuous indignation that a gangster feels when he learns that his spoils have been hijacked and his kidnaped prisoner has escaped.

3

Canada Retreats from the Empire and Europe

CANADIANS, as is to be expected of a small population inhabiting a huge area, are given to reckoning their achievements per capita. The world's fifth greatest foreign traders, they are per capita its greatest. That implies that they also have, per citizen, a relatively tremendous stake in world affairs, and particularly an interest in the maintenance of world peace. But if you asked them what influence they could bring to bear to shape the affairs of the world and keep its peace, they would probably answer that it is negligible.

The opposite is true. Per capita, Canadians could do little to provoke a world war but they could do more to avert it than the citizens of any other country under the sun. World wars cannot be fought without the participation of Great Britain, and Canada is in a position to exercise a decisive veto on British major wars. This is recognized by few Canadians and acted on by none. But it is a fact.

It is a fact because Britain can no longer fight a strong continental power or alliance of powers without access to the unrivaled industrial production of the United States, and in a lesser sense of Canada herself. For that access she needs three factors: command of the surface of the seas, willingness of the United States to sell, and an Atlantic harbor to act as the western base of a convoy system. Command of the seas depends upon herself. But she can obtain her western convoy base only from Canada. That is why Canada, when she took over the naval bases at Halifax and Esquimalt from Great Britain as part of her assumption of responsibility for her own defense, was required "to maintain them in a state of efficiency, provide storing accommodation for coal and other fuel for the Admiralty and dockyard facilities for His Majesty's ships visiting Canadian waters."

Without Halifax it would be almost impossible for the British Admiralty to convoy supplies from the United States. Britain has no other port that would take its place. Had it not been for the convoy system she would have lost the last war.

If Canada elected for neutrality in a British war she would have to deny the use of Halifax to Great Britain. For that matter, if Canada remained aloof, the United States, to judge from the prewar insistence of Congress on strict neutrality, would probably embargo the export of war essentials to Europe. Canada's abstention from the conflict would be an argument for the isolationists too powerful to be answered.

Canada, therefore, is an essential war partner for Great Britain. Australia, South Africa, or India could stay neutral without greatly affecting the issue, but without Canada the United Kingdom could not undertake a major conflict. And Canada, unlike Australia or South Africa or

India, could afford to stay neutral. She is protected by the Monroe Doctrine. They are not. No enemy in his senses would attack her for fear of adding the United States to his foes. That would hold true even if Britain were defeated. But if Britain goes down, Australia and South Africa and India go down too.

These facts are not cited to indicate the probability, much less the advisability, of Canada's abstention from a war in which Britain's existence is threatened. Canada could not stay out of such a war and stay in the British Commonwealth. And the British Commonwealth, however illogical and unwieldy, is worth preserving if only because it has demonstrated that a democratic Empire is possible, that autonomous nations can work together in a close partnership, that co-operation is a better solvent of national self-interest than coercion. It is a far more feasible pattern for that union of democratic states regarded by many as the only hope of peace than is the United States. The ability of Canada to dispense with war and the inability of Britain to dispense with Canada in a war are emphasized only to indicate how vital an interest Canada has in the shaping of British foreign policy and how decisive an influence she could wield in its determination.

But she wields no influence at all. For seventeen years she has refused not only to intervene in British foreign policy but even to be consulted about it. The poorest voter in London's East End has more control over Canada's foreign policy than a member of Canada's Parliament. The Canadian M.P. does not even know what it is until he reads the London dispatches in his morning newspaper.

Let scholarly authority curb exaggeration. There *are* some foreign affairs about which Canada does concern herself. Let us accept the summary of Canada's attitude toward foreign affairs compiled by Professors R. A. Mac-Kay and E. B. Rogers in their authoritative work *Canada Looks Abroad*. They write: "We are now in a position to summarize briefly the main principles of Canadian policy towards the Commonwealth as they appear to have been established during the years 1921 to 1930. . . .

"2. In order to avoid being morally committed to support by arms or other means imperial foreign policy in general, Canada now takes no part in the control of imperial foreign policy except where her interests are definitely at stake.

"3. Canada is prepared to consult and co-operate with Great Britain and other member-states of the Commonwealth in the formulation of foreign policy where Canadian interests are directly at stake. In such cases, the decision whether Canadian interests are at stake rests with Canada."

This conflict will be the third in which Canada has engaged since the outbreak of the Boer War in 1899. If it lasts three years—and it is being planned on that basis—Canada will have spent ten years out of forty-three fighting in imperial wars and will have added more heavily to her national debt because of them than for all peacetime reasons put together. If Canada is to spend almost a quarter of her time waging wars which are the outcome of imperial foreign policy it might seem that in the formulation of that imperial foreign policy "Canadian interests are definitely at stake." The last war, for instance, cost

50,000 Canadian lives and some 3,000,000,000 Canadian dollars.

The astonishing fact is that "in order to avoid being morally committed to support by arms" the imperial foreign policy which resulted in this war and which Canada is now supporting by arms, Canada's Government refused by so much as a whisper to approve, condemn, or amend it, while it was in the making. It even tried, with considerable success, to keep Canadian members of Parliament from discussing it.

Most students of foreign affairs agree that the implacable fates granted England and France their last opportunity to check Hitlerism without war when Germany reoccupied the Rhineland. There had been ample warning. Hitler's agents had sounded diplomatic opinion in Britain and France for weeks beforehand to ascertain whether France would answer reoccupation with mobilization, and whether England would guarantee her support. The possibilities of the move were known and discussed in the chancelleries before it was made. The challenge, as all the world knows, found France ruled by a weak interim government. Clemenceau or Poincaré might have decreed mobilization, secure in the knowledge that England, faced with the *fait accompli,* would have been obliged to support her ally. Sarraut could not find enough courage for independent action. He asked for England's aid. England demurred, advised against hasty measures. The opportunity was missed, and never recurred. Having reoccupied the Rhineland, Germany fortified it and then, secure behind her Siegfried line, devoured Austria, swallowed Czechoslovakia, annihilated Poland.

It would have been too much to expect the Canadian Government to intervene when Britain decided, for reasons that must now seem less convincing, to allow Germany to secure her western front. Canada had not signed the Locarno Treaty under which France thought Britain was pledged to resist that move. But Canada had fought a rampant Germany before and must expect to fight her once again. In the rearmament of so powerful an enemy, so openly dreaming of world conquest, at least that section of the Canadian public of military age might argue that it had an interest "definitely at stake." It might, under a democratic system, have expected from its government an exposition of the considerations that had influenced imperial policy in so critical a matter. It might, from its representatives, have expected some discussion of their merits.

But an attempt to air the matter in the Canadian House of Commons brought Prime Minister Mackenzie King to his feet in shocked protest. "I question," he said, "if there is anything we of this House could add which would be helpful to those who at this moment are involved in very critical and delicate negotiations on a matter of supreme concern to mankind. In the circumstances I think it would be in every way preferable, having regard to the extremely critical nature of the negotiations and the fact that the situation keeps changing not only from day to day but sometimes from hour to hour, for honorable members of the House to forbear, if they can see their way to do so, from preferring any request which might provoke discussion in this country at this time." In the event it was never discussed, not even when it was too late.

Encouraged by the results of her first overt breach of the peace treaties, Germany inspired the murder of Austria's little giant, Chancellor Dollfuss, stirred up a revolution in Spain, and then with Italy's help ensured that the revolution would succeed. On March 17, 1938, an Opposition member asked Mr. Mackenzie King whether Canada would remove her embargo on the export of war materials to Spain.

The Canadian Prime Minister replied that she would not and added: "We are witnessing momentous events on the continent of Europe. We are witnessing also momentous events on the continent of Asia. Canada lies midway between the two as a part of the continent of North America. Unless it is the desire to have it appear that our country is anxious to participate in these events, to become a party to or a part of what is happening on the continents of Europe and Asia, it is desirable, I believe, that all persons in positions of authority and responsibility in this country who have anything to do with the shaping and molding of public opinion, whether in Parliament or in the press, should refrain from taking any steps or making any representations which would appear to have a contrary aim or purpose. Moreover, I think we should be particularly guarded in what we say and what we do for the further reason that we should wish at all cost to avoid making the present appalling situation on the two continents more embarrassing for the countries faced with it, in their efforts to work out a solution."

Despite all Canada's reticence, the countries faced with it have not yet worked out a solution and Canada, for all her lack of anxiety to participate in these events, is now participating in them. The strictest observance of the taboo has not propitiated the dread spirits nor have thirteen years of tiptoeing around the sickroom prevented the corpse of peace from being finally stretched on her bier.

All the credit for Canada's hush-hush policy in foreign affairs cannot, however, be given to Prime Minister King. Mr. R. B. Bennett, former Prime Minister and then leader of the Conservative Opposition, joined with him in 1937 in opposing the creation of a standing parliamentary committee on foreign affairs. They gave many reasons but chief among them seemed to be that there were some things it was just as well to avoid discussing.

This ostrich maneuver when Empire foreign policy appears on the Canadian horizon may seem a strange behavior for a dominion which with its fellows was assured at the Imperial Conference in 1926 that they were "autonomous communities within the British Empire, equal in status, in no way subordinate one to another in any aspect of their domestic or external affairs." Sticking the head in the sand is a defective escape mechanism in that it leaves even more vulnerable parts of the anatomy exposed to eventual attack. Such a habit appearing in the behavior pattern of a country which has led the other dominions of the British Empire on the road to nationhood must obviously have something atavistic about it. And atavistic it is.

Deaf-mutism as a foreign policy had its origin thirty years ago and was invented as a defense mechanism by Sir Wilfrid Laurier when that great French-Canadian Prime Minister was defending Canadian autonomy against the cozenings of English duchesses and other advocates of a centralized empire, on the Kipling order. In 1902, declaring that "the weary Titan staggers under the too vast orb of its fate," Joseph Chamberlain had invited the dominions to take a share in the burdens of empire in return for a voice in the determination of its policy. Laurier offered to assume responsibility for Canada's defense but otherwise shunned consultation with the British Government on the ground that consultation would mean commitment. Canada, he felt, needed time to grow. The stripling nation should avoid the responsibilities of manhood until it had achieved the deep bass notes of maturity that would ensure it an equal hearing in Empire councils.

Sir Wilfrid Laurier was succeeded by a Conservative, Sir Robert Borden, who held different views. Like Laurier, he believed that Canada should assert her nationhood but he asked: "If Canada and the other dominions of the Empire are to take their part as nations of this Empire in the defense of the Empire as a whole, shall it be that we . . . shall have absolutely no voice whatever in the councils of the Empire?" When the war came he assented gladly to the establishment of an Empire cabinet consisting of five British cabinet ministers and the dominion prime ministers. It sat nearly every day to co-ordinate the Empire's war effort. At the Peace Conference the Empire War Cabinet was continued in a British Empire delegation. The dominions secured foreign recognition of their separate identity and in the League of Nations were given separate status and the right of election to the Council.

"If the self-governing dominions may not have adequate voice and influence in the direction of the Empire's foreign policy," said Sir Robert Borden in 1921, "it is not improbable that some of them will eventually have distinctive foreign policies of their own and that may mean separation." This common foreign policy, declared Lord Milner the empire builder, was to be "absolute out and out equal partnership between the United Kingdom and the dominions."

Canada made first use of her new dignity to intervene in imperial foreign policy in the interests of the United States. Mr. Arthur Meighen, who had succeeded Sir Robert Borden as Prime Minister, persuaded the British Government in 1921 not to renew the Anglo-Japanese Treaty, which, it was feared, might be resented by Canada's great neighbor. Canada's action made possible the Washington Conference a few months later at which Britain took the first steps toward the acceptance of naval parity with the United States. The United States in turn has since abandoned her insistence on freedom of the seas and thus have disappeared the two most serious potential sources of friction in Anglo-American relations.

Canada's first postwar intervention in imperial foreign policy had proved fruitful. But as the war and the comradeship in arms which had accompanied the war faded into the past, imperial consultation became formal rather than real. Then a year later came the unfortunate episode of Chanak. The Treaty of Sèvres, which Canada had signed, had awarded Turkish territory to Greece and established an international zone along the Dardanelles. But the Turks, who had refused to ratify the treaty, thrust the Greeks aside in Anatolia and threatened the inadequate British force guarding the Straits. Lloyd George cabled the dominion governments that the British Government would defend the Dardanelles pending new peace negotiations and asked if the dominions would send contingents, since their willingness to do so "might be a potent factor in preventing any actual hostilities." The substance of his appeal was announced to the newspapers before it was in the hands of Mr. Mackenzie King, who had taken office the year before. His reply was that the Canadian Parliament must decide so important a matter. New Zealand promptly declared that she would send a contingent but Australia followed Canada's lead. The incident passed off without war. Turkey won a new treaty and Britain, as the event proved, a new ally.

But the whole affair had left an unfortunate impression in the mind of Mr. Mackenzie King. Temperamentally cautious, he was confirmed in his suspicion that imperial consultation was unworkable. When the Treaty of Sèvres was succeeded by the Treaty of Lausanne, Canada neither signed nor helped negotiate it. In Parliament he admitted that Canada was technically bound by it as part of the British Empire but argued that Canada had no moral responsibility for its execution. When the Treaty of Locarno was negotiated in the fond hope that it would preserve peace by securing the Franco-German frontier against aggression by either of the countries which it separated, Canada had nothing to do with it.

Since Locarno, Canada has ceased in theory to be committed to British foreign policy when not consulted about it and has permitted consultation only when "Canadian interests were definitely at stake." Locarno, in the opinion of Mr. Mackenzie King, was not such an occasion, since it concerned "certain matters which are confined entirely to Europe." It has not proved an accurate analysis.

Mr. King soon found that his policy of resisting all advance commitments was compromised by Canada's membership in the League of Nations. The League, if it meant anything, meant collective security and collective security in its turn implied a commitment for mutual defense. Not even Sir Robert Borden, who believed in the League, had liked Article X of its covenant which obliged its members to guarantee each other's territorial integrity. It assumed, he objected, that the map of Europe had been redrawn at Versailles by the finger of God instead of the hand of man and that its new frontiers must be frozen forever by the threat of war.

But Mr. King's ground of objection to the League was far wider, as was made clear when he refused the Geneva Protocol of 1924. The protocol was designed to make disarmament possible by substituting a guarantee of mutual assistance and thus to find a way around French insistence that security must precede a real reconciliation with Germany. What Mr. King balked at was particularly "its rigid provisions for application of economic and military sanctions in practically every future war." He was against commitments, commitments in the Empire or commitments in the League, commitment to military sanctions or commitment to economic ones.

So intense was his determination that Canada must not risk war to avert war that in 1935 he repudiated the action of Canada's own permanent representative at Geneva. This was Dr. W. A. Riddell, lately counselor in the

Canadian Legation at Washington, now minister to New Zealand. A League embargo on the export of war weapons, credit, and certain key products to Italy and all imports from Italy had failed to halt the invasion of Ethiopia. And then Dr. Riddell moved in the Committee of Eighteen that oil, coal, and iron and their derivatives be added to the list. Why he did so without instructions from his government is a mystery to this day. It is believed in Ottawa that it was in response to the soft persuasions of the Eden group, which, feeling the ground already shaking under its feet, decided that this last daring move to equip collective security with teeth might find more support in London if it were made by a representative of the senior British dominion.

No oil for Italy meant no invasion of Ethiopia. The Italian Government promptly declared that oil sanctions would be considered an act of war. The Canadian Government almost as promptly declared that Dr. Riddell's action had "represented only his personal opinion and his views as a member of the Committee—and not the views of the Canadian Government." It added that "Canadian action and participation by the Canadian Government have been and will be limited to co-operation in purely financial and economic measures of a pacific character which are accepted by substantially all of the participating countries."

Not long after Dr. Riddell was transferred—and Mr. Eden was dropped. Just as the Chanak incident had frightened Mr. King away from Empire commitments, the oil sanctions fiasco convinced him that the League was also a danger. He declared in the Canadian Parliament that the

League should confine itself to seeking peace by conciliation, mediation, and removal of the causes of war, and
contended that League members, like members of the
British Commonwealth, should be able to reserve complete freedom of action as regards participation in wars
involving other members. The League, in other words,
was to be a debating society and a court of arbitration but
not a police force.

In retrospect the role played by Canada in the League
was not one which contributed either to peace or to security. Instead it strengthened the hands of those powerful
sections of British official opinion which have always con-
ceived the Empire in terms of power and distrusted the
League of Nations when it could not be made to serve
selfish ends. Not all the blame for this can be placed on
Mr. Mackenzie King and his Liberal governments. It was
a Conservative who condoned imperialist aggression when
Japan invaded Manchuria in 1931 and thus put the League
and the whole policy of collective security to their first
serious test. To do so he disobeyed the instructions of his
government and furnished the only known postwar instance in which Canada's representative has taken sides
abroad against the United States.

Mr. C. H. Cahan, Secretary of State in Mr. R. B. Ben-
nett's government, was the senior Canadian delegate to
the League Assembly of 1932. Colonel Harry Stimson,
President Hoover's Secretary of State, had proposed to Sir
John Simon, the British Foreign Secretary, that the United
States and Britain associate themselves in a refusal to rec-
ognize Japan's government of swords in Manchuria. Mr.
Cahan had been instructed by his own government to take

a stand which would have discountenanced Japan and encouraged such action as Colonel Stimson proposed. It is not known what induced Mr. Cahan to depart from his instructions—perhaps a talk with Sir John Simon, who had been complimented by the chief Japanese representative on having represented Japan's case before the League Assembly better than he could have done it himself—but the speech he made was of an altogether different kind. He hinted that China had not yet achieved a government that could maintain order in its territories, and commended to the attention of the Assembly Japan's claim that she had no connection with the "independence movement" in Manchuria, did not in fact want Manchuria except to preserve her rights and interests there. If this were true, the League pledge to protect its members against "external aggression" would, he pointed out, fall to the ground.

The repudiation of the League as an effective instrument of collective security by a Canada which had also refused to accept any commitments in the British Empire left the Dominion without a foreign policy. The League had been a godsend to the dominions because it had offered a means of reconciling differences about Empire relationship otherwise apparently irreconcilable. When the League, in the words of that distinguished Canadian editor, Mr. John W. Dafoe, "was ushered into the darkness with assurances of the most distinguished consideration by Mr. Mackenzie King," these differences returned. Mr. Dafoe predicted that it would leave only one alternative for Canada: "armed defensive isolationism and an external policy dictated by a single consideration—that of minimum risk and maximum security."

Actually Mr. King's government withdrew to the position that Canada must continue to avoid all advance commitments, even a commitment to neutrality in case of another imperial war, but must also arm against the unlikely event that she might decide to participate in another such war, which of course would be one in which Britain was "attacked." Mr. King agreed with Sir Wilfrid Laurier that "when Britain is at war Canada is at war," but maintained that it was for Canada's Parliament to decide the extent of her participation. Retreating from still another possible source of commitments, he declared that the time was not yet ripe for Canada to join the Pan-American Union.

When in the summer of 1938 war seemed to threaten over Czechoslovakia, Canada's Prime Minister was urged by imperialist-minded Canadian editors to declare that his country would be "ready, aye ready" to support Great Britain if she had to take up arms in defense of that pattern of democracy. He refused. Disillusioning events proved that Mr. Neville Chamberlain, so eager to find reasons for not defending Czechoslovakia that he even discouraged her from defending herself, would have been embarrassed rather than helped by such a *carte blanche* from Canada. Mr. King, of course, did not justify his inaction on that ground when it came up for debate in Parliament, but rather on the ground that the other dominions had behaved exactly as Canada had done.

. And then, on September 3, 1939, Britain and France declared war. On September 7, Canada's Parliament met in emergency session. Just before midnight on Saturday, two days later, it passed on division but without a recorded vote the Speech from the Throne requesting authority for the Canadian Government to take "measures necessary for the defense of Canada" and co-operate in the determined effort being made to resist further aggression and to prevent the appeal to force instead of to pacific means in the settlement of international disputes. Mr. Ernest Lapointe, Minister of Justice and chief representative of French Canada in Mr. Mackenzie King's cabinet, swung the House of ·Commons into all but unanimous support of participation in the war with a speech whose passion and eloquence recalled that delivered in a similar strain by Sir Wilfrid Laurier twenty-five years earlier. A non-participation amendment had been moved by two members of a group of French-Canadian nationalists but when it came to a vote only the mover and seconder and the leader of the Co-operative Commonwealth party (on personal pacifist grounds) signified dissent to the main motion.

Next day Canada made a formal declaration of war. While this was pending, Washington had taken the attitude that Canada was not a belligerent and therefore not within the scope of the United States war embargo. This friendly fiction was making it possible to rush across the border at the eleventh hour airplanes and other essentials which Canada badly needed for her own defense but had failed to obtain from domestic or British sources. The advantages of the situation were obvious. But Canada has a special caste of super-patriots who must have the form no matter what happens to the substance. "The Canadian force needs equipment," said the Toronto *Globe-Mail* editorially, "but not at the price of hypocrisy. We would lose the respect of President Roosevelt and the American people, and deliberately forfeit our own respect, were we to resort deliberately to subterfuge to get supplies."

This seemed something less than gratitude to President Roosevelt, who had made the subterfuge possible. But not even a President can come with impunity between some Canadians and their patriotism. No, nor a Governor-General. "A Canadian's first duty is not to the Commonwealth of Nations but to Canada, and those who deny this are doing, to my mind, a great disservice to the Commonwealth," declared the late John Buchan, Lord Tweedsmuir, in Montreal two years ago. He was promptly taken to task by that doughty champion of imperialism, whether Japanese or British, Mr. C. H. Cahan. Mr. Cahan seemed to think that Lord Tweedsmuir, the King's vice-regent, had been faintly disloyal to himself.

His hand forced by those who esteemed declarations above munitions as martial weapons, Prime Minister King declared war on September 10. But, unnoticed by the imperialists, he made this surrender to their demand the occasion for the tacit assertion of a new right of Canada to declare war of her own volition (and hence, if she saw fit, to elect instead for neutrality) which seemed to represent the greatest advance in her autonomy since the statute of Westminster transformed the British Empire into the British Commonwealth of Nations.

Canadian isolationists had frequently suggested that Canada, to round out her autonomy, should establish her right to remain neutral in British wars instead of automatically becoming a belligerent when Britain did. The legal-minded had objected that the Crown was indivisible, that the King could not thus be at war and at peace at the same time, that it would require action by the Imperial Parliament, and that such action would reduce the relations between Canada and Britain to a personal union like that which existed during Georgian times between England and Hanover.

Mr. Mackenzie King had declared in Parliament six months earlier that he did not think it desirable to take such action. It had been frequently suggested, he admitted, that the right of Canada to choose between the status of belligerency and the status of neutrality should be established, "or, as it is sometimes put, it should be established that the sole advisers of His Majesty who can advise him to issue a declaration of war as regards Canada are His Majesty's Canadian advisers." But he did not propose to do it because it could be "carried through only at the cost of passionate controversy and acute differences of opinion" and because it might bring "aid and comfort to any country which might be inclined to aggressive action against the democratic peoples or against the United Kingdom specifically."

But what Mr. King said he was not prepared to do he did. Not by invoking legislation from the Imperial Parliament nor even by provoking a debate in the Canadian Parliament. He did it by announcing in the House of Commons that the Canadian High Commissioner in London had been instructed to submit to King George "the petition of the King's Privy Council for Canada that His Majesty would approve the issuing of a proclamation in his name embodying the declaration: 'that a state of war with the German Reich exists and has existed in Canada as and from the tenth day of September 1939.'"

His Majesty had issued a declaration of war for Canada on the advice of "His Majesty's Canadian advisers." And there had been no passionate controversy or aid and comfort to the enemy. A few constitutional lawyers noticed it and said nothing. Newspapermen, including the writer, did not perceive its significance until long afterward. It is still news to the Canadian public. Mr. Mackenzie King had worked in most mysterious ways his wonder to perform.

4

Isolation Is Impossible
for Canada

CANADA'S foreign policy, as its history has indicated, has consisted, except for a Great War interlude, largely of a refusal to have any. This almost purely negative attitude has involved the surrender of any right to fashion in peace the imperial policies for which the Dominion has had to fight in war. It has retained for Canada, in her relations with Great Britain, a sort of technical virginity although, as the event has proved, an assignation had all along been foreordained for her on the battlefields of Europe.

This foreign non-policy was originated by Sir Wilfrid Laurier in the days when Canada had not attained her present stature, was interrupted by Sir Robert Borden and his successor Mr. Arthur Meighen, and was resumed by Mr. Mackenzie King in 1922. As Mr. King has been in office for twelve of the seventeen years since then, history will give the credit or blame for it to him. It is a product of his convictions and certainly a perfect expression of his temperament.

It has generally been interpreted as an assertion by Canada of the right to have a foreign policy of her own.

It was during Mr. King's regime in 1923, for instance, that his Minister of Justice, Mr. Ernest Lapointe, signed the Halibut Fisheries Treaty with the United States all by himself. It was the first treaty which Canada concluded without Britain's signing as well. Canada, it was then announced, had assumed control over her own foreign policy. The fact that Canada is now fighting a war ostensibly the result of a British guarantee to Poland in which Canada had no share is history's comment on this contention.

What was Mr. King trying to do with his policy of leaning backwards? It must logically be predicated on the assumption that Canada could abstain in fact as well as in theory from any war in which Britain became engaged. "I cannot accept the view," said Mr. King in the Canadian Parliament five months before the outbreak of war, "that regardless of what government or party may be in office, regardless of what its policy may be, regardless of what the issue itself may come to be, this country should say here and now that Canada is prepared to support whatever may be proposed by the government at Westminster."

Mr. King seemed to be reserving the right to veto the results of British tactics if he did not like them. What he meant was interpreted by his hearers to be that Canada might not fight in a British war of which she did not approve. "Go ahead," he seemed to be saying to Great Britain, "form your own policies and let us attend to ours. If you get into trouble because of them and we think you were right we may help you. If not, not."

This was a definition of his government's Empire relations that seemed to make sense. But a day later in the

same debate, Mr. King's chief lieutenant, Mr. Ernest Lapointe, declared apparently with the full approval of his
chief that Canada could not in practice remain neutral in
any British war. To do that, Mr. Lapointe pointed out
from the deeps of his considerable knowledge of constitutional law, would mean that Canada would have to forbid
the use of her harbors to British warships. Did anyone
doubt, he asked, that the attempt to do so would cause
riots on Canada's Atlantic or Pacific coasts, where loyalty
to the British connection has long been a tradition? None
doubted, not even Mr. Lapointe's discomfited French Nationalist fellow-members. It was a reasoned and convincing speech, which made hash of their isolationist convictions. The fact that it also made hash of the whole foreign
policy of Mr. Lapointe's leader did not seem to be noticed.

But if Canada cannot remain neutral in British wars,
obviously nothing is left of the policy of "no consultation,
therefore no commitment." Canada is still committed to
fight in any war in which Britain needs her assistance. She
is committed by circumstances, she is committed by her
traditions, she is committed by her emotions. None could
doubt it who saw drought-stricken Saskatchewan send her
children over three hundred miles of dusty road, in rusty
trucks that had not been able to afford license plates for
three years, and with money scraped up in parish bazaars
and school-house festivals, to wait for hours in a hot sun for
a brief chance to wave a Union Jack at King George and
Queen Elizabeth. French Canada may not like it, and
French Canada may be right, but French Canada must lump
it. Canadian loyalty to Great Britain has survived even the
Chamberlain government. Perhaps it sees Britain with a

time dimension in which the grant of South African autonomy cancels out the Boer War, the defense of Luck-
now distracts the eye from the massacre at Amritsar, and
the younger Pitt balances Mr. Baldwin. More likely it does
not see but just feels. It does not seem to matter.

What does seem to matter is that Canada, by refusing a
voice in the formulation of imperial foreign policy to
which, willy nilly, she is committed, fails in her duty to
herself, to Great Britain, and to the United States. In the
present war the consequences have been disastrous. Nazi
Germany is a foe far more terrible and menacing than was
imperial Germany. The Germany of Kaiser Wilhelm embodied all that America disliked and resented about Europe. She meant mailed might, truculence, and the wor-
ship of war. But at her worst she was only dangerously out
of date, a worshiper of old outmoded gods, a humorless
survival from a medieval age. Powerful and ominous, she
was yet earnest and God-fearing, and though she dreamed
of power over the bodies and territories of her enemies
she meant no menace to their souls. More important, she
represented no direct threat to America. But Nazi Germany is a creeping madness, a plague of the mind. She is
possessed by a vampire dynamism that must slake its thirst
at the throat of the whole world and fill the veins of all
humanity with the virus of its own delirium. And at her
back, available at the price of a final capitulation to Communism, is the world's greatest potential armory, Stalinist
Russia.

If the two should make common cause and win, it is
obvious that only armament for a generation on a scale
hitherto undreamed of on this continent can secure the

safety of the Western Hemiphere. Nor will eternal armament be the whole price of safety, for totalitarianism in
Europe and Asia will call forth totalitarianism in the
Americas. Isolation may be feasible but it will be terribly
expensive.

If the American people stay out of this war after intervening in the last one it can only be that they were dis-
illusioned by the results of their intervention. It is too
late now to discuss the peace fiasco or the undeniable mis-
handling of the otherwise debatable issue of war debts.
History may always have something to say on both sides of
those questions, and a section of American public opinion
has persistently doubted whether by repudiating President
Wilson the United States washed her hands of all blame
for what has followed. But if the course of British policy
in the past seven years had been deliberately calculated
to remove such doubts and generally to alienate American
sympathy it is difficult to see how it could have been improved upon.

"I have always thought," said Lord Lothian in 1934,
"that the mistake of British policy at the time was its rejection of Mr. Stimson's offer to reverse the isolationist
decision of 1920 and act with us in support of the collective system in the Pacific. This failure on our part to live
up to the spirit and the letter of the Washington treaties
early in 1932 drove the United States back into isolation."
Lord Lothian is now British ambassador to the United
States, and has more cause than ever to regret the rebuff
administered to her by that frigidaire of foreign secre-
taries, Sir John Simon.

Britain's failure to associate herself with the United

States against Japan's rape of Manchuria marked the end of collective security and the beginning of her long course of truckling to Fascist violence. Canada, which eleven years earlier had intervened in British foreign policy against the Anglo-Japanese Treaty, this time raised her voice against her own neighbor. In 1921 she had pressed home the American case against the decided reluctance of Britain, Australia, and New Zealand to sever relations with Japan. There is little reason to doubt that if she had been inspired by a similar determination in 1932, she could have secured a similar result.

Mr. C. H. Cahan, who condoned instead of condemning Japan's inauguration of a new reign of violence in Asia, has since sought to excuse Britain's rebuff on the ground that Colonel Stimson proposed nothing but a gesture. It is not apparent how this alters the case, since if the United States intended merely a formal protest Britain would risk nothing by associating herself with it and if, on the other hand, she were prepared to support intervention with sanctions, Britain and the cause of collective security would have found a welcome ally. Britain has certainly not found one since in Japan.

It is true that Mr. Cahan disregarded the instructions of his government when he defended aggression. But his action was not repudiated, whereas three years later, when another Canadian representative at Geneva proposed effective sanctions to halt spoliation in another quarter of the world, repudiation followed swiftly. It is impossible to say how large a part this played in the dropping by the British Government of the policy of collective action against Fascist aggressors and of Mr. Anthony Eden who

represented it. But its effect must have been considerable.
In one way or another, then, Canada did service to war-
makers.

After abandoning Ethiopia to Italy, England abandoned
Republican Spain to Franco and his Italian and German
allies. Austria was allowed to be sacrificed without a murmur and then came the humiliating pact of Munich and
its shaming sequel, the rape of Czechoslovakia. England's
prestige was now trailing in the dust. Her government,
apparently disbelieving in the existence of democracy, saw
no alternative to Communism but Fascism, and made a
series of abasing compromises with it which were repaid
with lies, insults, and fresh outrages.

Canada's pride was cut deep. But the truth could not
be admitted. Fiercely her newspaper editors defended Mr.
Chamberlain's retreat from Munich on the ground that
England had disarmed and could not fight. They forgot to
point out that he had been in successive Tory governments
since 1931, had been Prime Minister since 1936, and must
bear the responsibility for disarmament if it existed. Even
fiercer was Canadian resentment of the criticisms of England's policy expressed by American editors and radio
commentators. Why should the United States criticize
Britain when she did nothing herself?

It seemed to strike no one that, if Britain were having
a bad press in the United States, Canada could not escape
responsibility for it. Canada was supposed to be the interpreter between Britain and the United States, yet her
government had never raised a voice in disapproval of
Britain's disastrous foreign policy or pointed out the
calamitous effects it was having on American public opin-

ion. They might have realized that this was unfair to the
British people, who would be the chief sufferers if their
government's policy of making the world unsafe for democracy deprived them of the support the American people
had given in the last war. Obviously the greatest service
Canada could do for the British Empire would be to see
that when enemies threatened its line of march it did not
get out of step with its great natural ally. Only Canada
could do it. Her influence had been decisive in the reconstruction of the Empire after the loss of the American colonies: now it should be decisive in its preservation. "The
present British Commonwealth," wrote John Dafoe in
Canada: an American Nation, "resulted from the adop-
tion of successive expedients for the purpose of keeping
Canada in the family: this is the plain fact, simply stated."
"We realize," said Mr. Neville Chamberlain in 1937, "that
by our partnership with these other great democracies [the
dominions] we are raised from the status of a fourth-rate
power to be the heart of an Empire which stands in the
front rank of all powers in the world." Not since 1912,
when the dominions were invited to send ministers to represent them in the Committee of Imperial Defense, had
Britain sought to deny them a voice in foreign policy. It
was the dominions, led by Canada, which had held back.

In justification of his policy of consultation and no commitments, Mr. Mackenzie King had urged that it preserved Canadian unity. In the hearing of this writer he
pointed out how the device had served to bring Canada
united into this war. When her Parliament decided that
she must participate the expected explosion of French-
Canadian resentment had fizzled out like a wet match.

When Premier Maurice Duplessis of Quebec tried to re-
light it for election purposes two months later he was
blown out of office by the backfire. Canada's course had
again been left to the logic of events and again it had
proved convincing. Commitments in advance, on the other
hand, would have stirred up resentments in advance.

This argument must await proof. The real test of unity
is not at the beginning of a war but toward its end. It will
come if and when a long, exhausting struggle demands
conscription, against which Mr. King's government has
pledged itself. The Quebec election result, in the opinion
of many qualified to know, was partly a tribute to the
common sense of French Canadians in discerning and rejecting an unscrupulous election device and partly a vote
against conscription. The Quebec members of the federal
cabinet had let it be known that they would resign if Mr.
Duplessis were elected. That would mean a general election on the issue of Canada or Quebec. If conscription
were to be averted this must be avoided. So ran the election appeal and there is no reason to doubt its effect.

From 1917 to 1922 Canada had a place and a voice in
the councils of the British Empire. There is no evidence
that this harmed Canadian unity. It led eventually to the
increase of Canada's commitments by adding to them
membership in the League of Nations, but this, far from
dividing Canadian opinion, proved the most useful possible device for uniting it. Mr. Mackenzie King abandoned
consultation because he thought that the Chanak incident
had proved it unworkable. But his critics say that it was
Mr. King and not the British Government that was to
blame. They say that he had absented himself in his con-

stituency, leaving only an emergency secretary in charge
of communications. Mr. Winston Churchill's invitation to
send a Canadian contingent to help guard the Dardanelles
arrived in Ottawa on Friday afternoon. Within the next
few hours replies had been received from the other dominions. But Mr. King was not reached by his secretary until
the following day, by which time Australia's reply had
already been published. Whatever the merits of the case,
an emergency like Chanak is unlikely to find a dominion
Prime Minister incommunicado more than once in a
quarter-century. Accidents happen in the best-regulated
families without breaking up family relations.

Actually neither the time lag of Chanak nor Mr. King's
insistence that Parliament ratify important decisions in
foreign affairs has any bearing on the real criticism of
Canada's relations with Great Britain. It is not swift decisions that Britain needs from Canada, it can be argued,
but assistance in charting the general course of imperial
policy and more particularly when it promises to affect
the relations of the Empire with the United States. The
Canadian public has been far better informed about
events in Europe of recent years than have the British
people. The "voluntary press censorship" that denied
Englishmen the knowledge that an American divorcee
threatened to become their Queen for a month after
Canadians had been informed of it by American news
agencies did not cease when the Chamberlain government
was seeking to justify the results of "appeasement." But
Canadians continued to get the sharp-edged truth about
it in the news columns of their newspapers, although the
editorial page of one metropolitan daily "thanked God for

Mr. Chamberlain" a few weeks before the outbreak of war on the ground that he had preserved peace. Canadians resent American criticism of Great Britain but the very fact that their ears are accessible to it gives them all the better opportunity to gauge the effect of British policies on their great neighbor. Official Washington discusses some things far more freely with a Canadian minister than with a British ambassador. It would seem that Canada's policy of isolation in between wars has been almost indistinguishable in its effects, if not in its intentions, from a blind and dumb subservience to British imperialism. She might at least have registered her reactions in London. Her disunity had been cited as an excuse for her nonintervention. It was just because a war was likely to find her divided, it might be urged, that she should have intervened.

She should not only have intervened in London but she should have sought every possible opportunity to make her influence felt in Washington. It has often been pointed out that whereas Canada is almost as dependent on close association with the United States as with Britain she has no basis for intervention in Washington. That is largely her own fault. She was offered one in the form of membership in the Pan-American Union but has feared to accept it. A few months before war began Mr. Mackenzie King declared in the Ottawa Parliament that the time was not yet ripe to consider it. But was the time not overripe? If Canada had entered this war as a member of the Pan-American Union it could only have helped, not hindered, her in her vital task of organizing the resources of the continent in aid of the Allied war effort. It pays, in

international as well as in private affairs, to be a member
of the same club. Certainly it would have made her participation far more significant.

Of the few formal obligations which membership in the
Pan-American Union would have imposed on Canada
there are only two which would have affected her role in
this war. Clause C of the Collective Security Convention
achieved at the Inter-American Conference for the Maintenance of Peace at Buenos Aires in 1936 obliged the
signatories "in the event of international war outside
America which might menace the peace of the American
republics" to consult regarding "the proper time and
manner in which the signatory states, if they so desire,
may eventually co-operate in some action tending to preserve the peace of the American continent."

Clause E of the Convention for the Co-ordination of
Existing Treaties pledged its signatories in the case of
war "to adopt a common and solidary attitude of neutrality" and for this purpose they "may take into consideration the imposition of prohibitions or restrictions upon
the sale or shipment of arms, munitions, implements of
war, loans or other financial assistance to the states in
conflict, but only through the operation of the domestic
legislation of the high contracting parties, and without
prejudice to their obligations under other treaties to
which they may or may not become parties."

These conventions were signed in the full light of the
knowledge that some of the signatories were members of
the League of Nations and as such might be called upon
to impose economic or even military sanctions against

other signatories which broke its Covenant. The position of Canada as a member of the League and of the British Empire would seem to be on the same footing.

Canada's Prime Minister also acts as her foreign secretary. She is represented in London by a high commissioner and the British Government has a high commissioner in Ottawa. Under Mr. Mackenzie King's governments high commissioners have been given few responsibilities and fewer powers. Dispatches from Ottawa are not forwarded through them and they are not mouthpieces of their government. Their actual work was defined some years ago by one critic as "an effort to combine the functions of a commercial consul with that of a general publicity agent, to these being added an occasional and irregular intervention in affairs of state."

They are allowed to be informed but not "consulted." The ideal candidate for the post of high commissioner would obviously be a gentleman with large ears but no mouth. The post of British high commissioner to Ottawa, at least in the early days of that office, would have required the possession of a very thick skin. The ministers of Mr. King's cabinets had been instructed that their rank gave them precedence over the representative of His Majesty's British Government and they enforced it on official occasions with what almost amounted to unseemly jostlings.

If there is to be co-operation between them the obvious need is for both Britain and Canada to be represented in each other's capitals either by a cabinet minister or a minister plenipotentiary. A cabinet minister would have

to change with a change of government. A minister plenipotentiary could be a career man like the present Canadian
minister to Washington, Mr. Loring Christie.

Aside from the presence of high commissioners in Ottawa and London, contact between Canada and Britain
has been maintained in time of peace by the attendance
of the Canadian Prime Minister at Imperial Conferences
in London every three or four years. The only change
made since the present war began has been to send Canada's Minister of Resources, Mr. Thomas Crerar, overseas
for a few months to acquaint the British cabinet ministers
from the other dominions with the potentialities of Canada's contribution to Empire war effort. Before Mr. Crerar
sailed, Mr. Mackenzie King made it clear that what he
would attend would be no imperial war cabinet nor even
an imperial war conference but merely a meeting called for
specific informative and consultative purposes. The major
feature of Canada's war effort, her air training scheme,
was arranged in Ottawa.

It was far different in the last war. The Canadian Government was permanently represented in London by Sir
George Perley, one of its own cabinet ministers. In addition an imperial war cabinet was organized, and Sir Robert Borden, then Canadian Prime Minister, made periodic
visits to England to attend its meetings. He was no silent
partner in its deliberations. Early in 1918 he pointed out
to his colleagues that the capture of Passchendaele by the
Canadian Corps with the loss of 16,000 men had been useless since the British Army had immediately afterwards gone
on the defensive, that many English corps commanders
were not properly protecting their positions, that certain

army commanders including the ill-fated General Gough
were inefficient, that British intelligence reports had been
found unreliable by the Canadian Corps. He complained
that neither the War Office nor Admiralty was utilizing
the best brains of the nation. On June 13, 1918, after he
had protested strongly against "incompetency, disorganiza-
tion, and confusion at the front," Lloyd George told him
that it was for the purpose of strengthening his own hand in
dealing with the High Command that he had summoned
the dominion ministers to the Imperial War Cabinet.

It is urged that this is a war in which machinery, more
than men is needed, that firing power and not heads will
count. If this is true then it is the Canadian Corps which
proved it twenty-five years ago. Thanks to its commander,
Sir Arthur Currie, and its artillery expert, General A. G.
L. McNaughton (now commander of Canada's only overseas division), it had a striking power which made it the
prototype of the highly mobile, highly armed army corps
of today. It originated many things including efficient
counter-battery tactics and daylight raids. Canada was not
only in the British Empire and in the Empire's war but it
was helping to run both.

But there is no imperial war cabinet in this war, no
Canadian minister in London, no Canadian Corps in
France. There is no United States in the firing line and, at
this writing, no prospect that there will be. Meanwhile,
behind Germany, Russia is copying Germany's tactics of
avoiding a general war while pushing here, pushing there
against small nations in the hope of half winning the battle before the battle begins. The United States, with the
old memory of war debts and the recent memory of

Munich, looks on with an apathy reinforced by repeated assurances that this is "a competition in boredom" which must end in an Anglo-French victory. Hitler has again succeeded in dividing his enemies. It can only be hoped that he will not succeed in his objective of swallowing them piecemeal.

5

The Ostrich Policy and
the Men Who Made It

IN DESCRIBING and criticizing Canada's steady retreat to political isolation after the World War it was
pointed out that this course, with all its immediate advantages and its ultimate dangers, had been largely determined by her present Prime Minister, Mr. William Lyon
Mackenzie King. What has been said of Canada's policy
in foreign affairs could equally be said of her domestic
policies, for these, too, bear his stamp. In domestic as well
as foreign, in economic as well as political matters, Mr.
King has been a consistent believer in *laissez faire,* and in
a world given over to contrary doctrines he has held true
to his creed and held Canada true to it.

It has been a remarkable feat and Mr. King, outwardly
the most colorless of all Canada's politicians, is actually
one of the most complicated and remarkable leaders she
has ever had. He fascinates because there is no accounting
for him. His tactics often seem futile and footling; his
strategy has almost never erred. He is the sort of leader of
whom men say, in a tone of exasperated surprise: "Hang
it, he *must* be good!" The surprise is because Mr. King
seems able to attain a positive result by adding up a num-

ber of zeros and the exasperation is because they cannot
understand how he does it. Two of the most brilliant per-
sonalities in Canadian public life were successively his
opponents. Neither against the rapier thrusts of Mr.
Arthur Meighen nor the saber blows of Mr. R. B. Bennett
did he ever seem to have any effective defense. But today
Mr. Meighen is in the Senate and Mr. Bennett is in England. Mr. Tom Crerar, who once seemed to threaten Mr.
King's political life at the head of an emerging Progres-
sivism, is now in his cabinet. The stranger asking to see
Mr. King's works might well be bidden to look about him
—and see his wrecks.

Mr. Meighen and Mr. Bennett were successively leaders
of the Conservative party and Prime Ministers of Conservative governments. Mr. King since 1919 has headed
Canada's other historic party, that of the Liberals. The
Liberal party has divided office with its Conservative opponents since Canadian Confederation was achieved in
1867 by their joint effort. Mr. King has led it to victory
three times. His detractors declare that it is to his luck
as much as his deserts that he owes his career. They recall
that he was born a grandson of William Lyon Mackenzie,
a Liberal revolutionary whose name will long be connected with Canada's struggle for responsible government.
It was Mackenzie who in 1837 led Ontario's rebellion
against the Family Compact by which those Tory exiles of
the American Revolution, the United Empire Loyalists,
leagued themselves with English governors to monopolize
wealth and power. This, they say, won Mackenzie's grandson the favorable notice of later Liberal chieftains. Had

the Liberal party not been disrupted by the conscription issue which divided Canada in 1917 Mr. King, they allege, would have had to wait longer than 1919 before being selected as its leader. His first term of office coincided with the end of the 1921 depression and the revival that followed. His third term, 1926 to 1930, was made possible, they assert, only by the electoral exploitation of a constitutional issue unwillingly furnished him by the then governor-general, the late Lord Byng. He was lucky enough to go out of office in 1930 just before the full fury of the Great Slump began to ravage Canada. He was lucky enough to come back again in 1935 just when recovery was on the way. His next election was fought this year during a war—never a likely occasion for swapping horses.

The luck theory may partly account for the fact that Mackenzie King has been longer in office than any other living British Prime Minister but there is a good deal to be urged against it. It might have seemed his hard luck rather than good luck, for instance, to be seeking office as a professed devotee of democracy, parliamentarianism, and freer trade in a world which appeared to be given over to authoritarianism, regimentation, and economic nationalism. Yet it was on that platform that he was elected in 1935. His opponent, Mr. R. B. Bennett, had given Canada the highest tariff in her history and placed on the statute books on the eve of the election the blueprint of a New Deal with an NRA for primary producers, compulsory unemployment insurance, regulated wages and hours, and a general substitution of control for competition. But Mr.

Bennett was defeated and Mr. King's old-fashioned policy
of Gladstonian Liberalism won his party the greatest majority in its history.

It was a result which seemed to reverse the whole current of the times and to be without parallel either in
Europe or in America. In domestic as in foreign affairs
Mr. King had again proffered a negative as against a positive policy and again been endorsed. It could be added
that he had opposed a negative to a positive personality
and again been preferred. For his opponent, Richard Bed-
ford Bennett, was a gallant fighter and a strong man who,
if the times demanded dictators, seemed cut to the very
measure of the times. He had won easy verbal victories
over Mr. King in Parliament and on the stump had casti-
gated him with a vigor before which the Liberal leader's
reasoned but wordy appeals seemed to pale their ineffec-
tual fires. As a campaigner against so dynamic a personality and so positive a policy Mr. King had seemed negative
and naïve. With too much intellect to be a demagogue,
too little fire to be an orator, too little hair and too few
mannerisms to be a spectacular or even a distinguished
figure, he seemed in comparison with Mr. Bennett to be
scarcely a leader at all. Still less did he sound like one to
Canadians who had for three years past hearkened to their
radios reproducing the golden voice of President Roosevelt.

But it was the mild, the conciliatory, the cautious and
colorless Mackenzie King who was chosen by the Canadian
people as they had three times chosen him before. And he
is still in office and seems likely to stay there. From such
facts there was only one conclusion to be drawn: cautious

Mr. King and his negative policies might or might not be good for the Canadian people but they suited the Canadian people. They suited them because the Canadians are a diverse and divided population inhabiting a country cursed by sectionalism. In the matter of foreign policy they do not know what they want and in domestic policy they want different things. As against a political rival with a positive and dynamic program either at home or abroad Mr. King always seemed the lesser of two evils. For if Mr. King knows what foreign policy he wants he has never said so and domestically he generally represents a return to the *status quo ante*. He offers the mixture as before, watered down if necessary. Only in trade matters has he shown a high degree of courage, energy, and initiative. He made a trade treaty with the United States in 1935 and a new one three years later. In 1937 he revised the Ottawa agreements which had converted the British Empire into a closed corporation and bound Canada tightly to it. A year later, to permit the negotiation of new Anglo-American and Canadian-American trade treaties, he surrendered some of the preferences Canada had obtained in the British market.

But even in those trade negotiations in which he shone Mr. King stood for past policies rather than new ones. Closer commercial relations with the United States had been the traditional Liberal policy. Mr. King's revision in 1937 of the Ottawa agreements made in 1932 merely loosened the chains with which his predecessor, Mr. R. B. Bennett, had sought to bind the British Commonwealth into a closed empire and restored its freedom to trade with all the world. Mr. King's commercial policies, then, have

been like those of Mr. Cordell Hull. They have been remarkable not for their novelty but for the persistence with
which they have been advocated. They have been notable
less for the degree to which they have been applied than
for the fact that, in a world which seemed to have deserted
them, they have been applied at all.

In Canada the French Canadian is divided from the
English Canadian, the West from the East, the pro-British
imperialist from the Canadian isolationist. No political
leader need hope for federal office unless he can obtain a
substantial fraction of Quebec's solid 65 seats or somehow
reconcile the high tariff East with the low tariff West. If
he challenges French Canada, as Sir Robert Borden did in
the conscription election of 1917, he must have all the rest
of Canada behind him and embarks at best on a dangerous experiment. If he woos Quebec too openly he may
lose Ontario with its strong North-of-Ireland-Orange-
Protestant and United Empire Loyalist traditions. If he
invites too close relations with the United States he may
get into trouble as did Sir Wilfrid Laurier in the reciprocity elections of 1911, when even Liberal businessmen
rose electrically to the cry: "No truck or trade with the
Yankees!"

Only a very strong man, and then perhaps only on his
appointed occasions, could steer a new and positive policy
past so many reefs. On all other occasions he would find a
dangerous opponent in just such a politician as Mr. King,
a "safe" if undramatic figure with an uncanny perception
of what the voting public does *not* want and the gift of
devising policies so moderate that they could be made to
appear all things to all men. Under Mr. King the Liberal

party—once known in Quebec as the "Rouge" party—has moved over to occupy both right and center. The Liberals have become the real conservatives of Canada, leaving the official Conservative party nowhere to go; it bids fair to share the fate of the Liberal party in Great Britain and to have to choose like it between absorption or fractional existence. Certainly its present position furnishes the most striking possible evidence of the luck or maneuvering ability of Mr. King. In this year's general election, which as a war election was fought on war issues, Conservatism left itself without a cause. It would have had much to say about Canada's unpreparedness for war and it is true that Canada was unprepared, but it is equally true that in this strange war it has not much mattered. In any event, by precipitating the election this spring, Mr. King left his critics no time to say their piece.

The only logical ground of opposition to the present government was to maintain that its participation in the war is half hearted, that Canada must substitute the draft for its present voluntary recruiting of soldiers, and must equalize war sacrifice by conscripting wealth as well as manpower. But the Conservative party, under its present leader Dr. Robert J. Manion, had also pledged itself against conscription. It presumably did this in the expectation of securing support in Quebec, which Dr. Manion might otherwise hope to command because he is a Roman Catholic and is married to a French Canadian.

This may have seemed a reasonable expectation at the time the pledge was made, since Premier Maurice Duplessis was in office in Quebec at the head of a Conservative government. But now Mr. Duplessis is out of office and a Liberal government is in power in the French-Canadian province. Conservatism is left bound by its pledge of no conscription while any hope of benefiting from it in French Canada has disappeared. The position it might have occupied in view of its imperialist traditions was instead staked out by Mr. W. D. Herridge, former Canadian minister to Washington. Two years ago Mr. Herridge broke away from Conservatism to stamp a new party of his own—the New Democracy—out of the ground and the failing purpose of the Social Credit party which he has absorbed. He advocated an Empire policy for Canada but one in which she is to give the leadership. He declared for conscription of industry, wealth, and manpower and advocated the immediate creation of an Empire war cabinet to announce the Empire's peace aims and organize it to win the war.

Mr. King, re-elected this year for another five-year term, will have been in power in both war and peace and retained office longer than any other Liberal Prime Minister, even his illustrious predecessor, Sir Wilfrid Laurier. He will soon have become to Liberalism what Sir John A. Macdonald, with his seventeen years of office, was to Conservatism. Mr. King's theory of Liberalism, then, is important. It is that Liberalism implies confidence in the collective mind. A dictator's error may be fatal to his people but in collective decisions the mistakes cancel out. Mr. King works his ministers hard, unloads detail and executive decisions on them, collects their views on every issue, molds them into a policy, and carries out that policy by the most conciliatory methods possible. Government to him is not a business but an art. He has definite views of his own, but is ready to carry out other views for the moment if they seem to be those of the majority. He can wait. His enemies say he lacks the courage to enforce his convictions. His answer, if he could be provoked to make one, might be that he gets his way in the end, even if the only force he employs is that of passive resistance. His personality and policies were vilified for three years by the dynamic, resourceful, and not too scrupulous Premier Mitchell Hepburn of Ontario.

Mr. Hepburn's first appearance in politics had been in 1926, when he was elected to the Federal Parliament as one of Mackenzie King's supporters, the first Liberal returned in forty years in the Ontario constituency of West Elgin. He owned a 550-acre farm and had been secretary of the county organization of the United Farmers of Ontario. He was elected again in 1930 and shortly afterwards assumed the leadership of the Ontario Liberal party. In 1934, after it had spent thirty-two years in the cold shades of opposition, the blue-eyed, boyish Hepburn, known from one end of Ontario to the other as "Mitch," led his party to power. Treating tradition as a springboard and red tape as so much string, he immediately attracted notice by repudiating, as extravagant, contracts which had been made by the retiring Ontario Conservative government with a number of Quebec power concerns on behalf of the Ontario Hydro-Electric Commission. When the investment interests tried to retaliate by refusing to buy Ontario loans he sold them to the people through the provincial savings banks. When the CIO spread across the border into Ontario during the era of the sitdown strike he denounced them vigorously and called on the Federal Government to send the Mounted Police against them. On the basis of this and his defiance of the power interests the Ontario farmers voted him into power once more in 1937. Almost immediately he compromised with the power companies. His Conservative opponents accused him of betraying the public. His followers, who during his first two years of administration had hailed him joyously as the incarnation of democracy and vigorous, old-time Liberalism, began to feel less sure.

But Mr. Hepburn seemed to feel as sure of himself as ever. He was also certain that he had no use for Prime Minister King, for whose cautious, careful ways he felt a congenital distaste. Though a Liberal, he leagued himself in unholy alliance with Conservative Premier Duplessis of Quebec against King. It looked like an effort to achieve the domination of Canada by its two principal provinces.

But in November 1939 Mr. Duplessis found himself out of office after a provincial election in which he owed his disastrous defeat to the intervention of Mr. King's government. Mr. Hepburn, after two years of cold-shouldering Mr. King, journeyed to Ottawa—it might as well have been Canossa—to effect a truce with his leader. A year earlier there had been Liberals even in Mr. King's own government who had coquetted with the idea that Mr. Hepburn might make a better leader than Mr. King. But Mr. King had waited and Mr. Hepburn, like everything else, had come to him. An interpreter of the collective mind is necessarily amorphous. That makes him hard to hit. Mr. Hepburn, like Mr. Bennett before him, must have felt that he had wasted his blows on a pillow, and wondered uneasily whether he had been cast for the role of a Desdemona rather than a Dempsey.

His reconciliation with Mr. King—made primarily to recant his opposition to the St. Lawrence Seaway, whose power Ontario now needs—proved to be of short duration. He induced the Ontario Legislature to pass a resolution censuring the Federal Government's prosecution of the war—and thereby played right into Mackenzie King's hands. The Prime Minister was waiting for an excuse to call a general election before criticism of his conservative war policy could gather head and his enemy gave it to him.

Like Sidney's moon, Mackenzie King has climbed the skies with slow, sad steps. Now he hangs aloft, pallid and alone. Since the disappearance of Mr. R. B. Bennett from public life, there has been no one in the Canadian Parliament who can hold his own against him. This is true although he is in no sense an orator, is a better expounder than debater, and so long-winded that he concluded his speech at the opening of Canada's war parliament in 1939 by reading fourteen stanzas of a poem by James Russell Lowell. Dr. Robert J. Manion, leader of the Conservatives and thus of the principal Opposition party, is a likable Irishman with a distinguished war record. He is a gallant fighter in the thick of an electoral campaign but lacks the profundity which Parliament requires. Mr. J. S. Woodsworth, head of the Co-operative Commonwealth Federation, under which tri-petaled flower of speech Fabian Socialism disguises itself in Canada, has been successively schoolteacher, minister of the gospel, university lecturer, social service worker, longshoreman, and politician. He is the descendant of United Empire Loyalists who left New York for York—now Toronto—and a generation later helped suppress the rebellion led by Mackenzie King's ancestor, William Lyon Mackenzie. And now Mr. King represents the *status quo* and Mr. Woodsworth the revolution. He is an earnest moral figure but a little more demagoguery, fire, and fury would make him a more effective leader of his party and antidote to Mr. Mackenzie King.

As things are, Canada's King reigns almost alone. Fate or his own political skill has successively removed from his path the dangers which threatened it. Canadians, like the English but unlike the Americans, do not change their leaders merely for the sake of change. The second term of a Canadian Prime Minister makes his third term more likely, not less. And now Mr. King is embarked on a fourth term to add to his fourteen years of office.

Was it fate or was it skill that made it all possible? Perhaps Mr. King would say it was fate for, like Hitler, he is reputed to consult the seers. Good fortune-tellers, according to Freud, can read the subconscious minds of their clients. Perhaps Mr. King has resorted to them merely to find out what was in his own subconscious, for there is no doubt that the source of his political success has lain less in his conscious convictions than in his instinctive appreciation of an electoral situation. He seems, again like Hitler, to be subconsciously in touch with the mass mind. Since that is an indefinite thing, Mr. King is indefinite, and since our subconscious yearnings are never admitted, Canadians withhold praise from Mr. King in a way that seems hard to reconcile with their habit of electing him.

Mr. Roosevelt has charmed most Americans and caused

the remainder to rage against him. Mr. King charms few Canadians but has excited violent dislike in the hearts of still fewer. He has been able to command the lifelong allegiance of Ernest Lapointe and with it the votes of French Canada. Mr. Lapointe showed his qualities twice at the beginning of this war. Once was when he rallied French-Canadian members of the House of Commons almost to a man in support of Canada's participation in the conflict. The other time was when he defeated the attempt of Premier Duplessis to get himself a new lease of office by convincing the electors of Quebec that the Federal Government's emergency measures were a menace to their minority rights.

Mr. King's nebulousness and gifts of conciliation have made it possible to assemble under the Liberal standard a party representing so many different points of view that it is almost a Parliament in itself. Eastern protectionists and western free traders, French-Canadian Catholics and Ontario Orangemen, monetary reformers from the prairies and members of Parliament from Montreal and Toronto who could with justice, if not propriety, be referred to as "the honorable member for the banks" or "the honorable member for the railroads," march—if they do not always keep in step—under his leadership. In private they murmur against what they call his half-heartedness, in Parliament they often talk against his policies, but when the roll-call comes they vote for them. And the policies, in turn, are flexible. Mr. King believes in free trade but practices moderate protection. In his best-known book, *Industry and Humanity,* he has set forth in emphatic language the need for industrial reform. "Wherever in social and industrial relations the claims of industry and humanity are opposed those of industry must give way." Individualism, he wrote, must yield place to collective responsibility. Workers must be given security by minimum-wage and maximum-hour controls, unemployment and sickness insurance, labor exchanges, old-age pensions, and maternity benefits.

But when Mr. R. B. Bennett left on the statute books in 1935 measures to establish a compulsory unemployment insurance system and regulate the wages and hours of labor Mr. King referred them to the Canadian Supreme Court after expressing the view that they were *ultra vires* of the Federal Government. The Supreme Court, and after it the British Privy Council, upheld him and tore the legislation to pieces. Mr. King announced that he would accomplish the same ends by agreements with the provinces but five years have passed and he has not yet been able to do so.

Mr. King is a believer in freedom of speech and of the press. But when Quebec, during the Duplessis regime, enacted its famous "Padlock Law" against anything which its attorney-general wished to consider Communistic—and Mr. Duplessis was the attorney-general—Mr. King's government did not disallow the law. He has often spoken darkly of the "money power" and nationalized the Bank of Canada —Canada's equivalent of the Federal Reserve system—presumably to cope with it. But the Bank of Canada, until the war broke out, pursued a course as blamelessly orthodox as the Bank of England. When Premier W. C. Aberhart of Alberta—known irreverently on the prairies as Bible Bill —sought to put Social Credit unorthodoxy in force in his province, and, when that proved impossible, to slash agrarian debts, Mr. King's government intervened quickly enough.

Mr. King, like Mr. Roosevelt, is a professed humanitarian but there the resemblance ceases. Mr. King has embodied his convictions in a book; Mr. Roosevelt has written his in the statute books. The President, although an aristocrat, is at home with the great public, knows how to use the press, to make the air waves throb, to live and flourish in the limelight. Mr. King is camera-shy. He will not allow himself to be directly quoted by interviewers. His conception of propaganda is a four-hour speech in Parliament. When publicity seeks him out he wants to go home. For three months after the outbreak of war he refused to hold a press conference. At times of crisis he likes to retire to his study in Laurier House in Ottawa (his town house, which was the gift of Lady Laurier, widow of his great Liberal predecessor) or better still to his summer home on a shoulder of Kingsmere Mountain.

From there the imposing new Federal Parliament Building, symbol of his responsibilities, shrinks to less formidable dimensions against the broad sweep of the Ottawa Valley. Pat, his wirehaired terrier and inseparable companion, gives a sympathetic bark before sitting down on his haunches to share his master's contemplative mood. To Pat his master is a god but the stranger would see a man of middle height and bulk, with a face sicklied o'er in repose with the pale cast of thought, illumined when animated by a somewhat shy and boyish smile. Communion with himself relaxes Mr. King, distance gives him perspective on his problems, the clear air gives him energy to cope with them. Refreshed, he strolls back to his study to seek counsel of his books—for he is an outstanding example of the student in politics—or to mingle with his guests, to whom he exhibits in private a charm that he cannot command in his public contacts.

This is the man who has remained at the head of affairs longer than any other Prime Minister still in power in the British Empire. Because of the prestige his long years in office have given him and because, for reasons already cited, Canada occupies a key position in the British Empire and on the North American continent, Mr. King's personality and policies are worth far more study than they have ever received. In a previous chapter the writer ventured some criticism of those policies. In the next chapter the endeavor will be made to ascertain where they are leading.

6

King of Canada

IN OTTAWA before the outbreak of war it was being
said and written that Mr. Mackenzie King, once a
Canadian nationalist, had grown more imperialist-minded
with the passing years. He was risking defection from the
ranks of his French-Canadian supporters by arming Canada and arming her obviously for offense as well as for
defense. He had co-operated so wholeheartedly in the arrangement and conduct of the royal tour that his enemies
accused him of neglecting the business of Parliament to
spend a month in shepherding Their British Majesties
across the continent and back again.

There was no doubt of Mr. King's determination to
associate his high office in the public mind with this first
appearance in person of the British Crown, now the sole
link that binds the Empire. Never did Their Majesties
descend from their car in the rear of the Royal Train
without finding their chief Canadian adviser waiting for
them, silk hat in hand. Once, in his haste to cover the
distance from his own car a hundred yards ahead of the
royal coach, he jumped off while the train was moving at
twenty-five miles an hour. A huge mounted policeman
clasped him to his bosom and prevented an accident. The
British Government had wished to send a British minister

to accompany the King and Queen. But Canada's Prime Minister insisted on being their cicerone, in the United States as well as in Canada. It was evident, as he beamed on them, that he took a semi-paternal pride in their success.

He had had a good deal to do with their being there and even with their being King and Queen. When Edward VIII confided to Stanley Baldwin that he was unalterably determined to marry Mrs. Wallis Simpson, the opinion of Mackenzie King was sought. He could say what Canadians would think of it. He would incidentally have a better appreciation than any other Empire minister of the effect on public opinion in the United States if the King of England were permitted to marry an American double divorcee or were, on the other hand, forced to choose between her and his Crown. Canada had a stake in the preservation of good Anglo-American relations as well as in the prestige of the British throne. Edward VIII, too, was not only Canada's sovereign; he was a Canadian landowner and had personal friends from one end of the country to the other.

But Mr. King for once was definite. He replied that Mrs. Simpson would not be acceptable as Queen of England. A few days later Canadians in the East and the West and the Farthest North gathered around their radios to hear Edward VIII bid a moving farewell to the subjects he was leaving for "the woman I love." Five months later thousands of them arose at five in the morning to listen to the broadcast description of the coronation of his successor. The clock was turned back a thousand years. The past was resurrected and dressed in velvet and ermine and breathed on by an archbishop and came to life. Where

Edward VIII was never to sit now sat by the grace of God
His Most Excellent Majesty George VI. England had a
King again and the Empire a link to bind it together. And
Mackenzie King, who had helped to bring this about, sat
near by and doubtless reflected how far the grandson of
William Lyon Mackenzie—who had led Canada's only rev-
olution against the British Crown—had come from the
days when he was a reporter on the Toronto *Globe*.

Almost exactly two years later King George VI and his
Queen, who had already made history by the strange manner of their accession, made it again when they set foot as
reigning sovereigns on the soil of Canada. They made it
for the third time when they visited the mighty nation
which, but for the shortsightedness of an earlier George,
might have been the center of a still mightier British
Empire.

"Where do you come from?" the King had asked an
Irish-American journalist on that famous first rest day of
the royal tour at Banff Springs, Alberta.

The journalist had dined well that evening. "From
Boston, Your Majesty," he replied. "You know—George
III?"

"Ah, yes," replied George VI with a smile. "Something
about tea, wasn't it?"

It was easy to smile now about that first Anglo-American incident, which, however vividly remembered in
American schoolbooks, is to Englishmen and even to English kings one of many old, forgotten, far-off things and
battles long ago. But something more recent troubled
George VI as he approached the American border. His
brother, whom he loved, had been very popular in the

United States. Mrs. Simpson was an American. Would these things be held against him?

But Mr. Mackenzie King reassured him. It would be, he said, as though George VI had succeeded George V, than whom no British sovereign had ever been held in higher esteem in the United States. The event proved that he was right. Both in Canada and in the United States the unprecedented royal tour was an unexpected success. King George returned to England surer of himself and surer of the loyalty of Canada, about which shortly before his coming dark forebodings had been expressed by other traveling Britons. It was good news for the British Government, which set a higher value on the importance of Canadian assistance than Canadians suspected.

Three months later Canada lived up to expectations by entering the war and supplying a back door through which American munitions and perhaps eventually American dollars might reach Britain. But in the very act of doing so, as has been recorded, Mr. Mackenzie King reduced the relations between the Dominion and the mother country from legal unity under an indivisible Crown to a personal union, like that which under an earlier King George existed between England and Hanover. In the opinion of Professors Percy Ellwood Corbett and Herbert Arthur Smith, collaborators in discussion of the subject in their book *Canada and World Politics* (Macmillan Co. of Canada), this would detract from the dignity of kingship, reduce the Crown in fact to "the merest symbol."

It is interesting to speculate on King George's feelings when, after his senior dominion had maintained for a week a state of pseudo-neutrality, he was asked for the first time in Empire history to sign on the advice of his Canadian ministers Canada's declaration of war. He must have reflected, as so many had done before him, that his Canadian Prime Minister was a very complicated and baffling man.

What he had given with one hand Mr. King had prepared to take away with the other. He had traded Canadian assistance in one more imperial war against a precedent which established Canada's right to remain neutral, if she chose, in some future conflict. His decision, this writer was assured later, was the product of impulse rather than calculation. But circumstances had conspired to make it a perfect precedent. For a week after Britain's declaration Canada, though she had prepared for war, had not declared it. Her non-declaration had been accepted by the United States Government as evidence of her neutrality. There had even been a curious sort of confirmation of it by Germany herself. Erich Windels, Germany's consul-general and plenipotentiary at Ottawa, had assured an interviewer from the Toronto *Globe-Mail* during the fateful week that Germany, as things were, would not attack Canada or vessels of Canadian registry.

Then Canada declared war and Dr. Windels was given his passports. Perhaps he had hoped for a different outcome, since Canada's Prime Minister was known to be a sincere pacifist. The writer only a few years ago heard two shrewd observers, one a political friend and the other a political foe of Mr. King, agree that if the issue of peace or of participation in another European conflict were again to arise he would go to the country and cheerfully accept defeat if need be as an advocate of peace. When he quoted the prediction to Mr. King in 1936 the Prime Minister smiled thoughtfully. "Who knows?" he said.

In the event, Mr. King did not go to the country but went to war. No one who knew him well could say that in doing so he had betrayed his own passionate pacifism. He had never concealed his conviction that it was the duty of a Prime Minister to carry out the wishes of his people, irrespective of his own personal beliefs, and Canadian public opinion was overwhelmingly, if reluctantly, in favor of Canada's participation in the war. But there could be little doubt that Mr. King's decision was made with mixed feelings. Had he not himself declared bitterly in Parliament five months earlier that "the idea that every twenty years this country should automatically and as a matter of course take part in a war overseas for democracy and the self-determination of other small nations, that a country which has all it can do to run itself should feel called upon to save, periodically, a continent that cannot run itself, and to these ends risk the lives of its people, risk bankruptcy and political disunion, seems to many a nightmare and sheer madness"? No one who heard him doubted that among the "many" the speaker included himself.

Perhaps, then, Mr. King's gesture in extracting from present participation the possibility of future neutrality was intended as a sop to his own convictions. There are many who would argue that it did not matter since Eire has declared her neutrality in this war and some South African ministers have urged that South Africa already possesses the right to do so if she wishes. As for Canada the vital point, they would maintain, is not what she can do but what she wants to do and since she has demonstrated that she wants to fight with Britain when Britain is attacked, why labor constitutional technicalities?

But what Canada does in a war, for reasons that have been elaborated, is far more important to Great Britain than what South Africa or even Southern Ireland does. In the last analysis they must stand or fall with Britain whereas Canada could choose to stand with the United States. As for constitutional technicalities, they have a way, as lawyers know, of building themselves up into constitutional rights and, as rights, of being acted upon. Canada may be fighting with Britain now but what will she want to do after another postwar disillusionment?

And there are authorities who do not believe that the substitution for Empire solidarity of personal union with its separate right to declare war or peace is any mere constitutional technicality. In the opinion of Professors Corbett and Smith, already quoted, personal union would be "separation with a façade of union" which would "crumble at the first serious crisis in the relations of the separate states behind it. . . . Formally in his capacity as King of Great Britain and Northern Ireland, the King would acquire rights or assume obligations as against himself in his capacity as King of Canada. . . . It is, moreover, safe to assume that the title 'British subject' would have to be abandoned by citizens of the Dominions."

It may be assumed that Mr. Mackenzie King—no lawyer but a student of constitutional law—had read the opinion of Professors Corbett and Smith and knew that the assertion by Canada of an independent right to make war or peace must attenuate almost to invisibility the link that held her to the Empire. But Mr. King's whole previous course had been leading toward isolation and this was only another, perhaps the penultimate, installment of it. He had asserted Canada's right to decide for herself matters of foreign policy which she considered of special interest to her. He had refused to help shape imperial foreign policy and reserved the technical right to decline to accept its consequences. He had refused to experiment with economic as well as political imperialism. On succeeding Mr. R. B. Bennett, who had induced the British Empire to bind itself into a closed corporation, Mr. King had promptly discarded the exclusive features of the Ottawa trade agreements. "A world trade policy, not an Empire trade policy, represents our point of view," he declared. "What we believe in is economic co-operation based on autonomous national fiscal policies for each self-governing part of the Empire which will leave all free to deal with their own tariffs."

Mr. King had carried his assertion of Canadian autonomy to the point of risking—or, as his enemies said, of exploiting—a clash with the Crown itself. After the general election of 1925 he found himself without a seat in Parliament and with a party which could command a majority in the House of Commons only by an alliance with the Progressive block of 24 members. He formed a government which had to be headed in the House of Commons by his chief lieutenant, Ernest Lapointe. After a brief, uneasy existence it faced defeat on Conservative party charges, supported by the results of investigation by a parliamentary committee, that there had been smuggling scandals in the Customs Department. To avert this calamity Mr. King asked Lord Byng for a dissolution of Parliament. Lord Byng refused, whereupon the Prime Minister sent him a letter of resignation.

Not for a century had a British sovereign refused his Prime Minister a dissolution. Lord Byng could urge, however, that he had granted a dissolution ten months earlier and that King was seeking a second one to escape an imminent vote of censure. He accepted Mr. King's resignation and invited the Conservative leader, Mr. Arthur Meighen, to try his hand at forming a government. Mr. Meighen had been a fellow-student of King at Toronto University. He had gone west, taught school there, entered politics, and returned to the East as a member of Parliament. His keen mind and brilliant oratorical gifts soon ranked him as the chief intellectual figure in the Borden government. When Sir Robert Borden, broken by the strain of the war years, resigned in 1921, Mr. Meighen succeeded him and held office until his government was defeated by Mr. King a few months later. Now, in 1925, he grasped at another chance of power. British and Canadian custom demands that a member of the House of Commons who is appointed to cabinet office must resign and be re-elected. Mr. Meighen did not dare risk an appeal to the people in the special circumstances and formed a "shadow cabinet" of acting ministers with which he carried on until he was defeated in Parliament a few days later. He then resigned and secured from Lord Byng permission to call a new general election. Mr. King complained that what had been refused to him had been

given to Mr. Meighen by an abuse of the royal preroga-
tive and made this the issue in the general election of
1926.

Lord Byng was a descendant of Admiral John Byng,
shot for his failure to relieve Minorca in 1757. As General
"Bungo" Byng he had led the Canadian Corps at Vimy
Ridge and brought it to a high state of efficiency before it
was given a Canadian corps commander. Because of these
things he had been created Lord Byng of Vimy and named
as Governor-General to Canada. An aristocrat and a sol-
dier, he was in practice one of the most democratic vice-
roys Canada had ever known and was very popular in the
Dominion. But since 1837 Canadians have never tolerated
the assertion of any but formal rights by the King's vice-
regents and Mr. King made such good use of the issue
with which Lord Byng had furnished him that he was
re-elected on it.

A few months later Lord Byng's term of office expired
and he returned to Britain. As the Crown's representative
he could make no reply to Mr. King's public complaint
that he had exceeded his prerogatives, and the grave has
since claimed him. To some of his personal friends, however, he privately confided his own version of the affair.
This was that Mr. King had come to him in deep dis-
tress after his defeat in 1925, asserting that his political
career was ended. Lord Byng had offered comfort and,
though the Liberal leader had lost his own seat and his
party numbered fifteen fewer members than that of Mr.
Meighen, had consented to his endeavoring to form a
government. He had stipulated—in a "gentleman's agreement"—only that if Mr. King should fail Mr. Meighen

should be allowed to try. When Mr. King's government failed to command the support of the House of Commons Lord Byng had proceeded to carry out his part of the agreement in the belief that Mr. King would also consider himself bound by it. Lord Byng's friends believed his version. The public—which never heard it—believed Mr. King.

While putting the Crown in its place and demonstrating that as far as British imperialism was concerned he was distinctly "not a joiner," Mr. King had also shown himself the most North American-minded of Canada's Prime Ministers. "We Canadians," he declared on one occasion, "are fortunate both in our neighbors and our lack of neighbors. One has only to be in a European country a day to realize how relatively fortunate a position it is and what folly it would be to throw it away." He was, after all, the grandson of William Lyon Mackenzie, who had fled as an exile to the United States and found refuge there for twelve years. His mother, Mackenzie's daughter, had been the great shaping influence in his life; so great that he has never put another woman in her place and, as his close friends know, still communes with her in spirit. He had received most of his education at Harvard and the University of Chicago. He had lived in Hull House as a student of sociology under Miss Jane Addams. From 1914 to 1917 he had directed an inquiry by the Rockefeller Foundation into industrial relations. He had relinquished the post then to fight the 1917 election in which Sir Wilfrid Laurier, on an anti-conscription program, was defeated by a coalition of Conservatives and Liberals headed by Sir Robert Borden. Mr. King had been offered a safe seat if he would align himself with the conscriptionist Liberals but he refused and went down to defeat. But two years later he succeeded Sir Wilfrid Laurier as head of the Liberal party and in another two years he was Prime Minister. He has gone oftener to Washington than any of his predecessors and he made Canadian history by sending a Canadian minister there in 1926. Significantly, his first official visit to Washington at the outset of his political career was to achieve a common Canadian-American front in a delicate matter of foreign policy. This was in 1908, the year in which Mr. King resigned as Deputy Minister of Labor to become a member of Parliament and—a year later—Minister of Labor in Sir Wilfrid Laurier's cabinet. After an exclusionist riot in Vancouver in which several Japanese lives were lost, Canada was negotiating a gentleman's agreement with Japan to restrict the number of visas granted to Japanese emigrants. As a result of King's visit to Washington, followed by a visit to London bearing confidential messages from President Theodore Roosevelt to Sir Edward Grey, a similar arrangement was made by the United States with Japan.

It was as a result of Mr. King's mission that President Roosevelt wrote Sir Wilfrid Laurier: "Believe me, my dear Sir Wilfrid, that it was a particular pleasure to hear from you and to meet Mr. King and that I feel the directness, simplicity, and good faith of such a communication is a happy omen for the future. . . . I am exceedingly pleased at the steps that have been taken to bring our several peoples into a closer and more friendly connection."

The friendly relations which he established with one Roosevelt Mr. King was able to duplicate with another almost thirty years later. It was under his regime that the late Lord Tweedsmuir, Governor-General and thus titular head of Canada, exchanged visits with the head of the American state in 1937. These relations have continued up to and during this war. So has that independence of action vis-à-vis Great Britain that had marked Mr. Mackenzie King's peacetime course.

In Parliament Mr. King had spoken a word for those who considered it a "nightmare and sheer madness" for Canada to "risk the lives of its people, risk bankruptcy and political disunion" to save a continent that could not run itself. He has shown a certain determination, now that the war has begun, not to risk Canada's manpower, solvency, and unity to any greater extent than necessary in its prosecution. The fact that Canada has only a division overseas instead of a corps may be attributable to the unusual form and limited extent of the war in its early stages, although there is ground for believing that the British Government would have been glad to accept a larger number of Canadian troops for service in other parts of the Empire. But there are the best of reasons for believing that Mr. King whittled the Empire air scheme, of which Canada was to have been the center, down to an almost purely Canadian enterprise on a more limited and less expensive scale. The British delegation headed by Lord Riverdale, which came to Ottawa in October 1939 to negotiate with the Canadian Government and delegates from Australia and New Zealand, talked freely of a scheme which, according to information given to this

writer by a member of Mr. King's own cabinet, was to cost
$700,000,000 in its first year of operation, and train 25,000
Empire airmen every year after it reached its peak in a
year or a year and a half. But after almost two months of
negotiating, what emerged was a scheme the whole cost
of which is to be $600,000,000, spread apparently over
three years. The airmen trained are to be practically all
Canadians.

A week before the announcement was made the Aus-
tralian delegates were on their way home. Before they left,
Australia's Minister of Air, Mr. James Valentine Fairbairn, had announced in a broadcast that Australia, besides fulfilling its quota under the Canadian scheme,
would in three years give complete training at home to
20,000 of its own airmen. Mr. Fairbairn gave a picture of
Australia's war effort. He spoke, by what seemed to be
some bad management on the part of the Canadian Broadcasting Corporation, only a few minutes after Colonel J. L.
Ralston, Canadian Minister of Finance, had reviewed Canada's war preparations. Canadians, who had a few days
earlier heard Premier Mitchell Hepburn of Ontario de-
ride Canada's war contribution on the ground that it was
so inadequate "Americans are laughing at us," had opportunity to compare it with that of Australia. The population of Australia is not much more than half as great as
Canada's but as reviewed by Mr. Fairbairn her contribution of men, ships, airplanes, and money seemed to be
equal where it was not superior. Australia, of course, is
not protected by the Monroe Doctrine and is subject to
a far more imperative need than Canada to arm for her
own defense.

Critics of Mr. Mackenzie King have seen reflected in his direction of Canada's war effort the same principles as inspired his peacetime participation in the British Empire. They discern in the metamorphosis of what was to have been an Empire air scheme into an almost purely Canadian effort his anxiety lest Canada emerge from the war committed irrevocably to the Empire as its permanent military air center. They point out that the wave of patriotic fervor which swept over the country once hostilities were declared, bringing a rush of youth to enlist and of age to contribute, has been gradually stilled until now in Canada there is little more excitement over the war than there is in the United States. Though they admit it has been difficult to remain at white heat over a war so strangely lackadaisical in its early stages, they blame Mr. King for swimming too strongly with the current instead of against it. They see loyal enthusiasm damped down to a level of apathy from which, perhaps, it can never be rescued and they suspect this suits Mr. King only too well. They realize, as the leading anti-conscriptionist of the last war, Mr. Henri Bourassa, recently pointed out to a friend, that whereas in 1917 all the Conservatives and half the Liberals were for conscription now all the Conservatives and all the Liberals are pledged against it—a significant change of attitude.

Whether or not all this criticism of Mr. King is justified, there is no doubt it exists. Whether it comes to a head depends largely on the progress and character of the war. Should London be badly bombed or the Allied efforts threatened with failure there would probably be a demand in Canada for a more active and extensive war effort. If this included conscription Mr. King would have either to resist or resign. In such an event a national government headed by Lieutenant Colonel J. L. Ralston would become a possibility.

The demand might come from outside the Liberal party and be resisted by it as a whole. If Mr. W. D. Herridge had been elected at the head of his New Democracy party he could have been expected to lead such a movement. Before he emerged into the open two years ago as the leader of a new party Mr. Herridge had shown remarkable ability as a behind-the-scenes negotiator and architect of political programs. He inspired the electioneering tactics that swept his brother-in-law, Mr. R. B. Bennett, into power in 1930. He devised the New Deal with which Mr. Bennett tried to snatch another success in 1935. Some shrewd political observers have since commented that if Mr. Bennett could have entered more wholeheartedly into his role and exacted better chorus work from his Conservative reactionaries he might have won. But while the head of the Conservative party was purring goodwill to all men its tail was lashing indignantly. And Mr. Bennett himself was not well cast for the part. He was a millionaire, presumably thinking his millionaire's thoughts. The more he sounded like Roosevelt, the more he looked like Mussolini.

After the defeat of Mr. Bennett and his resignation as leader of the Conservative party, Mr. Herridge made an unsuccessful effort to convince Conservatism that it had better stick to reform, since Liberalism had left it no place else to go. When it became obvious that he would not succeed he rose grimly to tell a packed party convention

that its platform was "bunk" and that it was on the road
to the extinction it deserved. Having read himself out of
the party Mr. Herridge tried to organize one of his own
on a reform basis. After hostilities began he transferred
the accent from economic reconstruction to all-in prosecution of the war, with Canada playing a large part not
only in the Empire's front line but in its councils.

In peacetime Mr. Herridge had helped his brother-in-
law give a practical demonstration of willingness and ability to achieve Canadian leadership in the British Empire.
It is fairly well known now that Mr. R. B. Bennett did
not so much sign as write the famous Ottawa agreements
of 1932 which made a closed economy of the British Empire. It was Mr. Stanley Baldwin and Mr. Neville Chamberlain who found themselves signing on the dotted line
with a pen which, when Mr. Bennett handed it to them,
might almost as well have been a pistol. Behind the scenes
when Mr. Bennett was remaking the Empire nearer to his
heart's desire was Mr. Herridge, then Canadian minister
to Washington. Though invisible, Mr. Herridge was not
intangible to the British negotiators. If Mr. Bennett by
any stretch of the imagination could have been considered
a velvet glove, Mr. Herridge would have been the iron
hand within.

The true story of the Ottawa Conference has never been
told. It began in London in 1930 when Mr. Bennett, with
Mr. Herridge at his elbow, demanded the construction of
a tariff wall around the mother country so that the dominions might be able to secure preferred entrance through
it. "Humbug," remarked Dominions Secretary "Jimmy"
Thomas rudely. But two years later a British delegation

found itself lured from its home base to a parley which, as eminent persons and custodians of the world's greatest import market, they confidently expected and amiably intended to dominate. They failed to recognize that their position contained two essential weaknesses. They knew nothing about tariffs. Having left Britain in search of an Empire pact they could not return home without one. They discovered these disabilities before the conference was over but their host had discerned them in advance and, with the assistance of Stanley Bruce of Australia, he proceeded to capitalize on his prescience. It was not their ultimatum but his that was accepted. Whether it was statesmanship or only good poker is still a matter of debate in Canada but it demonstrated that Canada could get her way, if she chose, within the Empire.

Barring a revolt from within his party or an attack from without, Mr. Mackenzie King is likely to be given opportunity to guide Canada's policies during this war and perhaps for some time afterwards. If this happens, it may be predicted that he will lead Canada far toward isolation. His peacetime policies have pointed unmistakably toward this goal. There has been a curious parallelism between them and the postwar policy of the United States. The United States was in the World War and might conceivably get into this one. But after the war she elected to dissociate herself from European affairs and refused to join the League of Nations designed to organize and maintain peace. Mr. Mackenzie King has imitated this policy as closely as was possible in Canada's different circumstances. He has held aloof from European and even from

Empire affairs. He detached Canada from all but formal participation in the League of Nations.

He gave the rudder a further twist in the direction of isolation even in the very act of declaring war. He has so far contrived that Canada's war participation shall not leave her committed to the Empire as Sir Robert Borden tried to commit her in the last war. If this is really his intention his chief difficulty may be the Canadian air training scheme, which seems to have appealed to the imagination of the public. Canadians are air-minded and, even if they were not, a tidal wave of applications for training has poured in from the United States, from nearly every part of the British Empire including Australia, and from Great Britain herself.

But Mr. King will feel that his re-election in 1940 by an even more overwhelming majority than in 1935 gives him an unmistakable mandate to pursue his wartime policy. So far as can be discerned from past performances and professions that will be a policy of limited liability. Canada will not, if he can prevent it, bleed herself white in this struggle. Any demand by Britain for new efforts will be carefully weighed in the light of its effects on Canadian manpower and finances. It will be as coolly considered as though it came from an ally, rather than automatically assented to in the spirit of "Who dies if England lives?"

This may well have been what Canadians voted for when they gave Mr. King's government its record majority, although he called the election before the war in the West had lost its trance-like character, or opposition to the alleged lukewarmness of his participation in it had had time to gather head. It is true Dr. Manion had tied his hands with a no-conscription pledge. Mr. Herridge, who alone championed all-in participation in the war, sought election and found defeat in a western constituency with a large foreign element among its voters. The war issue was not clearly defined, and while French Canada may have voted for the government in the belief that it was endorsing limited participation, many Canadians may have done so in the sincere conviction that they were giving a new mandate for active prosecution of the war. All these things must be admitted, but the fact remains that the Canada which gave Mr. King's "no conscription" government so tremendous a majority in 1940 had moved far from the position occupied by the Canada of 1917 which put a coalition government in power to enforce conscription.

If the war should end with a Franco-British defeat, isolation under American control will be forced on Canada. There are, of course, substantial reasons why the United States might intervene rather than let the Allies go under. If the war ends in a stalemate or an Allied victory, the disillusionment that inevitably comes with peace will leave Canada in a state of mind where isolation, if skillfully presented and persistently practiced, will become a fact even if not a theory. Idealists such as Lord Lothian have been talking of a postwar revival of the League of Nations idea. But Great Britain helped to lay the last League of Nations in her coffin and Mr. Mackenzie King pronounced a blessing over the grave. The sexton turned midwife would be more grisly than convincing. Even the most convinced believers in a policy of collective security for Canada would turn sadly from such a spectacle

and decide that it was too late to follow any other lead
than that of the United States into isolation. It would be
a continental policy which would leave Canada a satellite
of the United States where she might have been the key-
stone of a world-spanning English-speaking union. It would
mean that she rejected the great role offered her by history and decided on a policy of second best. If the United
States keeps out of this war she will be confirmed in
isolation.

To follow the United States into isolation will undeniably be the easiest way for Canada. But will it be the best?
Canadian champions of the policy argue that if the United
States ever wishes to coerce Canada her British connection will not save her and, conversely, that Mexico—with
no European protector—is able to flout American big
business today. Canada's relations with the United States,
they point out, improved from the very day she took
charge of her own affairs.

Actually, Mexico has been coerced in the past—there is
California to show for it—and may be coerced again. As for
preserving equality of bargaining power with the United
States, a Canada able and willing to represent the American viewpoint in the British Commonwealth is obviously
more useful to Washington than a country with a long
coastline and fewer people to defend it than Mexico. But
the tragedy of the situation, if Canada should drift out of
the British Commonwealth without even trying to make
it work, would be its serving of notice on the world that
one more great, historic experiment in international co-
operation had failed. If a British Commonwealth could not
endure, what price a federal union of the democracies?

PART II

*

Origins
of the Problem

7

Canadian-American Relations: A Stormy Record

IN CANADA, to be "disloyal" means to be disloyal to Great Britain. Such a crime as disloyalty to Canada scarcely exists. A Canadian may with utter safety impugn the motives of a Canadian government. He may deplore his country's attitude in this or that matter of foreign or domestic policy, disparage her past, or doubt her future. Few will answer him and none will question his right to revile or even to despair. But let him challenge the expediency of her present relations with Great Britain and he will bring a hornet's nest about his ears. Let him, for instance, argue that Canada's security depends in the last analysis upon the Monroe Doctrine rather than upon the British Navy and he will provoke a swarm of angry editorials in Canadian newspapers and a myriad indignant letters to their editors.

It will be worse for him if he attacks the policy and still worse if he assails the motives of any British government. If he does he may be denied space in many influential Canadian newspapers and he will certainly be denied the facilities of the Canadian Broadcasting Corporation. Before and after Munich a Canadian propagandist for the

Chamberlain government was allowed to explain away in a weekly broadcast from London those developments of its policy which had been troubling the souls of many inhabitants of this continent, north as well as south of the 3000-mile border. But when Mr. George Ferguson, editor-in-chief of that influential and independent western journal, the Winnipeg *Free Press*, ventured to embarrass the Canadian air waves with a reasoned criticism of the Chamberlain course there was indignant protest in the Ottawa Parliament and Mr. Ferguson was suppressed.

With very few exceptions no English-speaking member of either the Liberal or Conservative parties ever criticizes British governmental policy in the Canadian Parliament. A small group of French-Canadian nationalists does so, and so, sometimes, do the few members of the Co-operative Commonwealth Federation. They get little attention and still less publicity.

These conditions prevailed in peacetime. Now that there is a war they have become more acute. One could mount a soapbox in Hyde Park today and say things about the war and the British Government for which one would be promptly jailed if one said them in Canada, certainly if one said them in Toronto. Most of the few Canadians who, at the time of writing, have been fined or imprisoned for offenses against the Defense of Canada Act have sinned in this way.

The fact that Canada is in some ways more pro-British than Britain herself seems even more remarkable when it is considered that in many respects she is less English than the United States. There are, for instance, two official languages in Canada, French and English, as against only

English in the United States. Archaic English, the sort that men spoke in Shakespeare's time, is still to be heard in the Kentucky hills. The only archaisms in Canada are to be heard in Quebec, where the French Canadians have preserved some of the oddities of speech of their Norman ancestors.

The original thirteen United States were settled by the English except for a few Hollanders and Swedes. Canada was settled by French and Americans. Roughly speaking, it was still French at the time of the American Revolution. Its first considerable English immigration—as an Irishman would say—came from America and consisted of United Empire Loyalists, the Tories of America who fled north during and after the revolution of which they did not approve. More than half of Canada's population today is of other than British origin. And yet Canada professes Britannicism like a religion and—in those important respects which have been described—she practices it also.

To understand how these things are it is necessary to consider Canada's history. It is sometimes argued that Canada is largely an American product. So she is, but in the same sense as Protestantism was a product of Catholicism. The first English-speaking Canadians were protestants against the American revolution. They fled in fear and resentment; they lived in fear and resentment; slowly the fear has passed but the resentment remains. Modern Americans who, when they think of Canada at all, think of her only with the kindest feelings find it difficult to realize this. They might, indeed, point to the famous undefended border and the highly benevolent neutrality which the United States is now exercising—what might be described, in fact, as "neutrality for Canada"—as unmistakable evidence of their good intentions. So they are, but they must be set against a long past in which America was a menace to Canada and Britain her only source of safety. For nearly a generation it has been different, but a generation is not long in the history of even so young a country as Canada.

Canada was conquered by Great Britain in 1760. Before this, of course, the British had traded into Hudson Bay and there were small English settlements such as Port Royal—now Annapolis Royal—which had been founded in 1605, three years before Champlain reached Quebec. In 1776 came the Revolutionary War and the exodus of the Loyalists from the American colonies. Loyalists were tarred and feathered by Whig mobs, sometimes even murdered. Their property was confiscated. Two-thirds of the City of New York had been owned by Tories. Because this was so the British forces did not bombard it but they spared it, so far as the Tories were concerned, in vain. By the Treaty of 1783 which ended the war Congress undertook to recommend that the States restore the property of Loyalists who had not borne arms against the Revolution and allow those who had done so to repurchase their property within six months. But the treaty was not fulfilled, a fact which the 100,000 who had fled without their possessions into the lonely North never forgot or forgave.

Most of these Loyalists settled in Nova Scotia, New Brunswick, and Ontario. They stamped into the soul of Canada certain characteristics which time has not erased. They left her a legacy of distrust of the United States. They gave her a conservatism which is perpetuated today in her respect for law and order and, less fortunately, in her comparative unprogressiveness. They were Americans themselves but, because they resented the new Republic and all it stood for, they must necessarily revere the British connection and all they had withstood for it.

There was a curious ambivalence in their attitude toward their new country. Those of them who had been merchants, landowners, and army officers gathered around the English Governor of Upper Canada—now Ontario—took political control, and through their monopolization of place and privilege brought about the Rebellion of 1837. But most of them were farmers, workmen, and soldiers. They had been affected, perhaps without realizing it, by their American environment and they made common cause with later emigrants from below the border of whom Governor Gore was to write in 1808 that "the residue of the inhabitants of this colony consist chiefly of persons who have emigrated from the United States and of consequence retain those ideas of equality and insubordination . . . so prevalent in that country." They and their descendants helped Canada win that independence (only Governor Gore would have called it insubordination) which she has attained. But though they were ready to contest the issue of autonomy with English governors and governors-general to the bitter end, they remained utterly British. This may be a paradox, yet it has a parallel in Northern Ireland, which was prepared to take up arms against the Asquith Government in 1914 to resist Home Rule but has at all other times proclaimed and practiced a fierce loyalty to Great Britain.

The distrust and dislike of the United States which the

United Empire Loyalists brought with them to Canada
were intensified rather than allayed by the events of the
next hundred years. Europeans to whom the long, undefended Canadian-American frontier is cited as an object
lesson have sometimes sought to explain it away as being
due to the absence of hostile tradition between the two
countries. Actually, in the one hundred and fifty-seven
years of their separate existence, Canada has twice been
invaded by the United States and within the last seventy
years the territory of each country has been used as a base
for guerrilla attacks against the other. If now for one
hundred and twenty-six years there has been peace between them, they were near war three times and as late as
1895 Canadians had almost resigned themselves to hostilities over the Venezuela boundary dispute.

The first American attack on Canada was the "friendly
invasion" during the Revolutionary War when General
Montgomery occupied Montreal and then united with
General Arnold in an unsuccessful siege of Quebec. The
second was during the war of 1812, which Canadians have
always believed was begun as a pretext for the conquest of
their country. This, in the words of that eminent Canadian Sir Robert Falconer, was "a war which should not
have been fought, Britain did not want it nor did New
York, and the New England States were so bitterly opposed to it that they talked of seceding from the Union."
But Henry Clay had urged that "it is absurd to suppose
we will not succeed. I am not for stopping at Quebec or anywhere else but I would take the whole continent from her
and ask no favors." Andrew Jackson said it would be a
"military promenade."

As in 1776, Americans had miscalculated the strength of Canadian resistance. Canada put into the conflict every man capable of bearing arms. The Loyalists, who, rather than sacrifice their principles, had fled from the United States a quarter-century earlier, now found themselves forced by the country they had abjured to take up arms and defend themselves. And desperately they did it. Though invading American forces burned York—then the capital of Upper Canada and now Toronto, capital of Ontario—and Commander Perry won victories against British vessels on the Great Lakes, the United States armies gained little glory and no territory in Canada. The Treaty of Ghent, which ended the indecisive struggle and heralded a century and a quarter of what John Dafoe has called "peace with friction," did not determine a single one of the issues of the war. Neither, unhappily, could it remove the bitterness—now doubly confirmed—of the Canadians. The United States, they feel, tried to do to them in 1812 what the Germans did in 1938 to Austria. It was the "geo-politics" of that time. Americans are, of course, taught that war was over the interference with American commerce and impressment of American seamen.

It was a Canadian revolution which produced the next cause of friction. Originating in resentment against the Family Compact between autocratic British governors and the ruling clique among the United Empire Loyalists, it ended as a struggle for responsible government. The rebellion, both in Upper Canada and in French-Canadian Lower Canada—where its origins were partly racial—was easily suppressed. As usual, those who escaped hanging as rebels got what they had rebelled for. In this category was William Lyon Mackenzie, the York editor who led the revolt in Upper Canada. Taking refuge on Navy Island in the Niagara River after an unsuccessful attack on his home town, Mackenzie proclaimed a provisional government and hoisted a flag bearing two stars and a new moon. A thousand Americans rallied to his side and threatened the Canadian border. There were "incidents" and more "incidents" and soon the whole frontier bristled with bayonets and bad feeling. The American Federal Government stepped in decisively in 1838, but not until 1842 was the danger of war removed. Mackenzie was imprisoned in Rochester jail for nearly a year, found sanctuary in the United States for a decade, and then returned to Canada and became a member of the Canadian Parliament.

The next talk of war between Canada and the United States was in 1844, when James K. Polk was elected President after a campaign for American occupation of the whole of Oregon with the soothing slogan "fifty-four forty or fight!" In the end, the forty-ninth parallel became the boundary and there was no fighting but both nations had begun to prepare for it before the compromise was achieved. War was nearer still two decades later because of the resentment felt in the Northern States over British sympathy with the Confederate cause and the use of Canadian territory by Confederate agents with raiding designs against the North. This was complicated by abortive Fenian invasions of Canada from American territory in 1866 and 1870. It was fear of the United States that caused the Canadian provincial leaders to sink their sectional differences in a pact of Confederation in 1867. Had not

the American Government urged that Canada be annexed
as compensation for British violations of neutrality during the Civil War and terminated the 1854 Reciprocity
Treaty with her as an economic measure to force her
hand, it is doubtful whether Confederation could have
been achieved.

The last occasion when war with the United States
seemed possible to Canadians was in connection with the
dangerous Venezuelan boundary dispute of 1895. Canada
had nothing to do with it but she realized that Britain
and the United States could not clash without involving
her. If she had any doubts on the subject Secretary Olney's
invocation of the Monroe Doctrine in the case of Venezuela and his assertion of sovereignty over the whole
American continent would have removed them.

There have been many other causes of disputes between
Canada and the United States; the history of Canadian-
American relations until very recent times is largely, in
fact, the story of their quarrels. The last American President remembered with bitterness by some Canadians is
Theodore Roosevelt for his forceful handling of the Alaskan boundary dispute in 1903. This dispute originated in
the difficulty of determining just how much territory the
United States had acquired by purchase from Russia.
Canadian historical authorities have since admitted that
the United States had a very good case. But it was not
recommended to Canadians at the time by President
Roosevelt's statement that Canada's claims for a Pacific
port for her Yukon trade had been manufactured to get
her in on the gold rush to Alaska, were "an outrage, pure
and simple," and that the Canadians "acted in a spirit of

bumptious truculence." Even the conciliatory Sir Wilfrid Laurier was led to say in Parliament: "I have often regretted, and never more than on the present occasion, that we are living beside a great neighbor who, I believe I can say without being unfriendly to them, are very grasping in their national actions and who are determined on every occasion to get the best in any agreement which they make." For a long time the Alaska Panhandle looked as illogical to Canadians as the late Polish Corridor to Germany.

Fisheries were another fruitful source of contention. By the Treaty of 1783 which ended the Revolutionary War the United States was given the right to fish on the Newfoundland Banks, in the Gulf of St. Lawrence, "and also on the coasts, bays, and creeks of all other of His Britannic Majesty's dominions in America." Persistence in the assertion of these rights, which impaired the sovereignty of Canada and Newfoundland, troubled Canadian-American relations for more than a century. "What right," asked Daniel Webster in 1852, "have those distant and petty provinces to deprive our fishermen of privileges which they have enjoyed since 1818?" A reason why Canada generally emerged from treaty as from boundary negotiations with the feeling that she had obtained the short end of the stick was that, whereas the Americans acted for themselves, British negotiators acted for her until very recent times.

There could be two views, of course, regarding the part Canada played in all this. At a Canadian-American educational conference at the University of Maine in 1938 Dr. Harold A. Innis of Toronto University declared that "the nuisance value of Canada in Anglo-American relations has been neglected as a subject of investigation. It was Great Britain and the United States that had the will to peace and Canada cannot escape the accusation of playing the role of the small boy anxious to stick pins in either when there was something to be gained by it. It is only with maturity that Canada can be expected to play a role in which pin-pricking will cease to be a policy, in which we will cease fishing in troubled waters, and in which we shall take advantage of the 'will to peace' between Canada and the United States. The weakening of nationalism, the strengthening of regionalism, and the stress of imperialism leave Canada as the weak link in the North American structure—the Achilles' heel to North American isolation."

The Canadian-American "will to peace" has now found expression even in tariff relations. It was high time. The trade agreement of 1935 was the first that could be made after seventy years of tariff hostility. It was the only one of its kind in the history of the two countries with the exception of the 1854 Reciprocity Treaty, which met its death in 1866 as one of the international victims of the American Civil War. Canadians complained bitterly in 1866 of its abrogation. They have since complained bitterly of the high duties their goods have had to pay on seeking access to American markets. Yet they rejected reciprocity in 1911 when they could have had it. Rejection was the sequel to a remarkable flag-waving election in which the economic issue was completely beclouded by invitations to annexation in the United States and in Canada by appeals to "loyalty" and even to religious prejudice.

"It is her own soul," wrote Rudyard Kipling, "that Canada risks today. I see nothing for Canada in reciprocity except a little ready money that she does not need and a very long repentance." In Canada the issue was put more succinctly as "No truck or trade with the Yankees!" When reciprocity was defeated, one Canadian newspaper declared that Canada had "decided against continentalism in trade or politics." Canada, of course, had done nothing of the kind. She had merely added to her traditional distrust of the United States, even when bearing gifts, her distrust of her own ability to keep relations with her magnetic southern neighbor on a strictly business basis if she should enter partnership with him. The verdict was a reflection not only of her desire to remain British and virtuous but of her feeling that she might not be able to resist the temptation to do otherwise if exposed to occasions of sin. It was, in fact, a last flare-up of colonialism. As John Dafoe put it to the writer, "In 1911 Canada still had a boss. There was always the chance that she might change him for another and therefore an issue to be made out of preventing it. But when she began to feel grown-up and her own boss it narrowed down to a question of selling goods or not selling them."

Since 1935 the Canadian-American tariff question has practically been taken out of politics in Canada. Although the 1935 treaty was made by Prime Minister Mackenzie King, like the revised one three years later, it was first sought by Mr. R. B. Bennett just before he went out of power in September 1935. This meant that the party which had opposed reciprocity in 1911 and declared its platform to be "high protection and loyalty toward England" had turned wooer for closer trade relations with the United States. Since those closer relations have become a fact there has been virtually no criticism of them, either in Parliament or out. So far as Canada is concerned, a leading irritant has disappeared from Canadian-American relations.

The disputes over boundaries, fishing, and navigation rights which plagued the earlier history of Canada's dealings with the United States have also become things of the past. This is due principally to the Rush-Bagot Treaty of 1817 which abolished armaments on the Great Lakes and to the devisement in the International Joint Commission of a machinery of adjustment that has achieved a remarkable record of reconciliation since 1912. The disappearance of war vessels from the Great Lakes removed a fruitful cause of "incidents." The dismantling of their forts was like the substitution of a smile for a frown. Psychologists say that to practice a smile is to come to mean it. Even though this smile was a little forced at first it broadened eventually into the famous undefended frontier. Only once, in 1864, did the United States threaten once more to show her teeth. Notice was actually given to the British Government to legalize an increase of armament to stop apprehended Confederate raids from Canadian territory. It was approved by a joint resolution of Congress. But next year, the scare having died down, it was withdrawn. The undefended frontier had become unique —a world's wonder that time could not wither but only make more wonderful. Both nations had grown too proud of it to wish to see it sacrificed.

The International Joint Commission has been the active agent where the undefended frontier has been the passive agent in promoting good Canadian-American relations. It is, like the frontier, unique. Authorized in 1909 as a body to adjust international border questions which previously could be solved only by diplomatic negotiations or in troublesome cases by reference to an outside tribunal, the Commission was organized in Washington in 1912. In the ensuing quarter of a century it has amply realized Elihu Root's desire "to dispense with the Hague Tribunal as far as concerns matters between the United States and Canada and set an example to the world by the creation of a judicial board as distinguished from a diplomatic and partisan agency." It has never divided on international lines and rarely divides at all. It has a common background of law and a common interest in the preservation of boundary waters, especially the Great Lakes, center of the world's greatest industrial area.

The Commission made all boundary waters and canals connecting them free to both countries and prevented their diversion or pollution without common consent. But any matter may be referred to it, so that in practice it constitutes a permanent international tribunal for the adjudication of any dispute between Canada and the United States. Once referred, the dispute is decided according to law and justice. Even where the Commission's aid was not directly sought it has helped by creating a tradition of amicable settlement whose results were obvious, for instance, in the compromise reached in 1929 over the sinking in the Gulf of Mexico by an American coast guard vessel of the Canadian rum runner, *I'm Alone*. For a time prohibition in the United States and the tendency of the

Canadian frontier authorities not to be curious about the destination of liquor exports threatened good relations. But in 1930 the Canadian Government decided that good neighborliness required it to honor the spirit as well as the letter of the law and since then the two countries have achieved a degree of co-operation in the prevention of smuggling and crime found nowhere else in the world.

Canadian-American co-operation was closest of all in the World War when Canada's Atlantic coast was for a time patrolled by American cruisers against the threatened U-boat menace and American seaplanes helped to man flying stations at Sydney and Dartmouth, Nova Scotia. There was admiration in the United States for Canada's war achievements and in Canada a feeling of relief that her great neighbor had made common cause with her. After the war, although this was apparently never realized in the United States, these good relations gave way in the Dominion to irritation over the American attitude toward war debts, war glory, and the League of Nations. Amusingly enough, Canada's resentment was excited chiefly by a series of articles in an American magazine of national circulation assessing the United States' share of credit for defeating Germany at a degree considered high in the Dominion. What made it amusing was that the writer of the articles was born in Canada, and was the brother of a Canadian provincial premier.

But as the World War receded into history and the disappointing nature of its results became all too obvious, it quickly ceased to be worth while disputing who had won it. The American attitude toward its legacy of debts was resented for a time in Canada but when Britain stopped paying them there was nothing left to resent. If there had been it would have disappeared in the crash of 1930 when the erstwhile "Uncle Shylock" lost his own money and Canada and the United States became bedfellows in a common adversity. And then came President Franklin D. Roosevelt with his deliberate cultivation of good relations with Canada as part of a good neighbor policy and his promise of protection against the growing menace in Europe. Canadian-American relations reached a pitch of friendliness that they had never known except during the two years when the nations fought on the same side in the same war. There was something febrile about that wartime emotion that doomed it to end with the conflict itself. But the new basis of good feeling between Canada and her southern neighbor promises to survive even a war in which she is engaged and her neighbor is neutral. She has rejected isolation for herself, though she shows no disposition as yet to question its propriety for the United States.

8

Is There a Canadian Nationality?

THE previous chapter reviewed the historical events which have helped shape the attitude of Canadians toward Americans. They are to be found in the schoolbooks, and though the average Canadian has forgotten them they have played their part in determining what might be called his "official" view of the United States. Some Canadians of an older generation remember them all too vividly.

Such a one is Mr. C. H. Cahan, who liked Americans so little that at Geneva in 1932 he gave aid and comfort to Japan against the wishes of the United States and his own Government. At the ripe age of seventy-nine Mr. Cahan is still a distinguished, active, and able figure in public life, and a fine old crusted specimen of the Canadian Tory. He could generally be relied on, when Canadian-American tariff negotiations were under way, to help matters along with a speech reflecting the darkest suspicion of Washington's motives and probable intentions. When Secretary Hull visited Ottawa and Toronto a few years ago the first thing that met his eye in a Canadian morning newspaper was a speech of Mr. Cahan's assailing his whole trade policy as a series of Machiavellian devices. "Who is this

Cohen?" Mr. Hull is reported to have asked, a remark which, if Mr. Cahan had heard it, would have been ample revenge on that Aryan Presbyterian.

Mr. Cahan cannot forget, as he admitted in the Canadian House of Commons in February 1939, Secretary Olney's contention in 1895 that 3000 miles of ocean "make any permanent political union between a European and an American state unnatural and inexpedient." Nor can he forget, as he said on the same occasion, President Theodore Roosevelt's comments on Canada's case and motives in the Alaskan boundary dispute. Fortunately a younger generation of Canadians not only can but does forget.

They have done that despite the schoolbooks, which in Canada as in the United States have ministered to patriotic pride and national self-consciousness at the expense of historical objectivity. In the terms of peace which will end the present war should be a clause providing for the preparation, by an expert committee under the League of Nations, of standard historical textbooks for all the world. The Daughters of the American Revolution would probably object to it in the United States, and the Daughters of the Empire would certainly do so in Canada. But the proposal would find wellwishers in both nations. Dr. Louis Bénézet, Superintendent of Schools for Manchester, New Hampshire, would doubtless be one of them, since he remarked in 1938 to a Canadian-American educational conference: "Although Mr. Richard Rush and Sir William Bagot did a good job in 1817 they should have gone a bit further. Somebody should have been appointed to censor the textbooks in the two countries. I once got hold of a Canadian history. I was amazed to find how little I knew about what had happened in 1812. I had thought that the forces of the United States had won every battle. They didn't at all. They won very few battles. And I had thought that Winfield Scott or General Brown were the heroes of the war. I had been taught in my school histories what a heinous crime it was for the British to burn the Government buildings in Washington. That fact was not given. On the other hand it told how the Yankees had gone over and burned the Government buildings in York, now Toronto. I could not believe it was the same war until I looked up the date."

But heartening evidence was produced at the same conference that the influences of geography can outweigh the heritage of history. Mr. H. A. Davis of Columbia University related how he had lived in Calais, in Maine, where it borders New Brunswick. Across the St. Croix River, which is the boundary between Maine and New Brunswick, is the Canadian town of St. Stephen. For Calais and St. Stephen the boundary line—defended or undefended—might just as well not exist. They draw their water from a common source ten miles behind St. Stephen; Calais, apparently without finding the fact remarkable, is thus the only American town to derive its water supply from a foreign country. The gas and electric light systems are also operated in common. The fire companies on either side of the river answer each other's calls and race to see who gets there first. An appalling decrease in the Calais birthrate was traced by the county health officer to the hospital in St. Stephen, advantage of whose superior facilities was being taken by expectant Calais mothers in blissful ignorance of the complications of nationality to which they were exposing their prospective offspring.

Shades of the Webster-Ashburton Treaty! Thus does the man in the street—at least on this continent—work out his own formula of good neighborhood if given his head. The boundary that King William of the Netherlands found it impossible to determine to the satisfaction of Maine in 1831, the boundary that Maine ten years later was ready to fight over, he adjusts in the essential matters of life to suit his convenience and his common sense. He can do this because across that boundary he sees a man he can barely distinguish from himself. Canadians and Americans are more alike than any other two separate peoples in the world. That is not strange, since the inhabitants of the Maritime Provinces of Canada are to a large extent descended from New England Loyalists, the St. Lawrence and Great Lakes region of Canada was peopled partly from New Hampshire and Vermont and the province of Ontario from New York State. When the good citizen of St. Stephen crosses the St. Croix to Calais he finds himself among people more like him than, say, the inhabitants of Victoria, British Columbia. And the brave burgher of Calais, crossing to St. Stephen, feels more at home than he might in New Orleans. He may have kinsmen there; he is virtually certain to have them somewhere in Canada.

It has been calculated that two young people who married in Canada fifty years ago would be fairly certain to have half their descendants living in the United States today. Families have flowed across the frontier and back again. There was a Canadian-born member of President

Wilson's cabinet. There was an American-born member of Mr. R. B. Bennett's cabinet and there is another in Mr. King's cabinet. Colonel Lindbergh's mother was a Canadian. Among his brothers and sisters the writer numbers both American and Canadian citizens.

When the first Conference on Canadian-American Affairs was held at St. Lawrence University (Canton, New York) a few years ago under the auspices of the Carnegie Endowment for International Peace, it revealed what might well have been predicted, that there was very little the conferees had to learn about each other. They were, of course, far better than an average sample of the public of their respective countries. But from the first they spoke each other's language and found it necessary to make few allowances for each other's viewpoint. Their discussions, if sometimes vigorous, were always couched in the same idiom. This identity of mental processes was taken as a matter of fact by those who shared it, but it astonished M. André Siegfried, the French economist who has been a close student of Anglo-Saxondom. He had attended many European conferences, remarked M. Siegfried, but none where there was such a complete lack of fundamental difference, such a marked feeling of continentalism, as at this one. A British journalist returning from Canton contrasted it in the writer's hearing with the Ottawa Imperial Conference of 1932, where the inability of Canadians and Englishmen to comprehend each other's viewpoint had been as notable, he thought, as its antithesis at Canton.

Visiting Britishers, finding so little that is recognizably English about Canada or Canadians, are apt to go home and there to view with alarm the "Americanization" of the senior Dominion. Actually what they see and hear merely reflects the fact that Canadians, like Americans, have lived for almost two centuries on the North American continent and have reacted similarly to the same continental influences. In dress, manner, and social customs it is natural they should resemble each other. Take the important matter of pants. An Englishman calls them trousers, has them cut half-way up his back, and supports them with what he calls braces. The Canadian, like the American, calls them pants and, as often as not, belts them tightly just above his hips. Given almost any provocation he will discard his waistcoat, which he knows as a vest. He drinks more rye than Scotch, more hard liquor than wine, likes two crusts on his pies and dislikes Brussels sprouts and boiled puddings. If you prick him he will not only bleed like an American but swear like one. He prefers baseball to cricket, likes his football rough, shoots golf at par instead of bogey. He spends little time in clubs but is a great joiner of fraternal societies. He leaves his lot unfenced, builds verandas on his houses and sits on them in warm weather. He says "Say" instead of "I say," "Lookit" instead of "Look here," pronounces "aunt" as though it were a small, creeping creature, and says "thought" like "thawt" instead of—oh, well, the way the English pronounce it. He shows the same strange tolerance of calf-like crooners and turgid after-dinner orators, the same esteem for the arts of salesmanship, the same belief in laws rather than law, the same attitude toward organized labor, the same essential Puritanism of outlook, the same dread of Communism and belief that it is only an importation, to be shut out like a noxious drug.

He has the same individualist philosophy as his American cousin, is like him a great driver of automobiles, owner of telephones and frigidaires, and a gadget-user generally. He organizes his business on American lines, is almost as fond of stock gambling, much less given to having "five bob on the favorite in the 2:30," than his English equivalent.

One of the reasons why a Canadian is so like an American is that sport, religion, radio, the press, and even business in North America are so largely organized on continental rather than national lines, with the United States the dominant source. A quarter of the news in Canadian newspapers is about the United States, and American regular and special services provide much of their information about Europe. Canadians listen to more American radio programs than to Canadian and English combined. Apprehension caused by this fact in the minds of Canada's political, religious, and educational leaders led to the creation of the government-controlled Canadian Broadcasting Corporation. Hollywood supplies their films. Canadian Methodists, Baptists, and Irish-Catholics have close affiliations across the border and most Canadian trade unions are international. So are hockey and baseball, and there was a time when more Canadians followed the fortunes of Notre Dame than of any one football team of their own. Higher educational facilities have been almost interchangeable. Canadians have the same faith as Americans in the advantage of education for all. They cherish the same belief that there is nothing degrading in a boy's working his way through college, whereas in Britain only in London University has anything of the kind been known.

As against these powerful influences tending to identify Canada with the United States, Canadian unity has been preserved partly by fostering a protective prejudice against' the American idea. This has been aided both by Canadian and American tariff seekers. If American politicians have twisted the tail of the British lion, Canadian politicians have often found it good business to twist Uncle Sam's coat tails. Americans have been denounced as materialistic, politically and juridically corrupt, lawless and cynical about it, given to murdering each other and shamelessly neglecting to commit adultery before seeking divorce. Although the United States has nearly always felt friendly toward Canadians—even when she wanted to annex them it was in their best interests—Americans have often been unfriendly to Great Britain and that has irritated Canada.

Canadians understand Americans as individuals much better than they understand Englishmen as individuals. No signs reading "Americans need not apply" have ever been seen over the doors of Canadian offices. But together with the fact that he likes the Americans he knows and knows more Americans than any other people, the Canadian is able to keep in his mind in a separate, watertight compartment an image of the United States which he dislikes. For that matter he has been able in the course of history to remain violently loyal to Great Britain while waging a relentless if generally silent battle with the British Government and its representatives in Canada for more autonomy.

The matter, on examination, seems to belong in the domain of religion rather than politics. The Canadian has wished to save his soul, or in other words his identity. The

United States represented the temptations of this world, the primrose path to broad markets, the easiest way to security, the sinful delights of a high living standard. Great Britain had made Canada in her own image, been her help in ages past, still pointed the way to salvation, and was conveniently remote. So Great Britain was deified and the United States was equipped with horns, cloven hoofs, and a tail. In the course of time Canada has ceased to fear her god or hate her devil but their images have retained a strong symbolic significance. They are still stock figures in Canada's political demonology, which can be taken out, dusted off, and used with good effect among the faithful.

One of the things which has made it difficult for Canadians to achieve toward the United States that attitude of easy friendliness which makes a man or a nation a good neighbor has been that Canadians know so much about Americans that it is difficult for them to realize how little Americans know about Canada.

They are surprised and offended when they fail to find any mention of Canada in American newspapers although their newspapers are full of news about the United States. Their sense of humor fails them when the inevitable American tourist from California appears at the border in July with skis and a sled lashed to the back of his car. In his mind's eye every Canadian has a map of this continent on which his country is shown to be occupying a slightly larger half than the United States. It is difficult for him to be broad-minded about the sublime indifference to this fact he sometimes encounters south of the border.

His quarrel appears to be principally with the American newspaper press, which, with the exception of the New York *Times*, has never taken half the trouble to report Canada that it has taken with Mexico or Argentina. This is partly because its coverage of Canada is continental, a matter for the telegraph rather than the foreign desk. Canada has been handled, in effect, like just another American State, and on such a basis it is seldom able to compete. Its criminals are fewer and show a lack of dramatic sense; its big shots are generally beaten to the draw by the law. Two-fifths of its people, being Roman Catholic, sue for no divorces. Its political scandals are either of lower horsepower or are better covered up; its political changes are made more gradually. How can Mr. Mackenzie King, who admits that he dislikes publicity, hope to compete for the front page against the crowd appeal of magnetic Mr. Roosevelt? On top of all this, Canada, with its thinly peopled spaces, its sectionalism, its two official races, and its British-Americanism, is complicated and difficult to sum up in a headline. Statistically, it is easy to demonstrate its importance to the United States but its light has been hidden under the bushels and the company reports of the market pages of the American press where it has been permitted to shine at all. If happy is the country which has no history, then Canadians should rejoice, for their country has no history in the United States.

When 1200 high school seniors in the United States and a similar number in Canada were tested regarding their knowledge of each other's country a third of the Americans declared that Canada was ruled or owned by Great Britain. "Canada is no country," wrote one of them. "It is just a province of England." Only three per cent of them had ever heard of that charter of peace, the Rush-Bagot Treaty. One of them put the situation in a nutshell.

"Canada is so close and yet so far away from me," he wrote. "I know less about it than almost any other place in the world."

It was not their youth alone which accounted for the ignorance of Canada's status shown by the 1200. As late as the year 1923 the United States Senate attached a reservation to the Halibut Fisheries Treaty which Mr. Ernest Lapointe had signed for the Dominion, indicating that the Senate believed Canada to be a part of Great Britain. This displeased Canadians more particularly because this happened to be the first treaty a Canadian minister had ever signed directly on behalf of his own country instead of for the Empire.

President Arthur A. Hauck of the University of Maine, who told the 1935 Conference on Canadian-American Affairs at Canton, New York, about the results of the high school test, told them also that he had examined all the commonly used American textbooks in history and geography. While the war of 1812 had been discussed at length by all but two, the Rush-Bagot agreement was mentioned in only five histories, the International Joint Commission not even in one, and the achievement of Canadian Confederation in only six. A series of widely used textbooks for junior high schools scarcely mentioned Canada.

English Canadians are far more like Americans than they are like French Canadians or Englishmen. But there are subtle differences. Canadians take their work more calmly and their pleasures more sadly. High-pressure salesmanship never threatened to blow off the cylinder heads in Canada. High-pressure radio announcing is not favored, as one announcer discovered when he tried it during the Moose River Mine disaster in Nova Scotia some years ago. Canadian theater audiences are among the world's coldest. A political convention in the United States bears the same relation to a political convention in Canada as bedlam bears to a cemetery.

Canada, although she abolished titles some years ago, is less thoroughly democratic than the United States. There is more reverence in the Dominion for authority and for the great. A parliamentary committee which wanted to take some evidence from Sir Herbert Holt during a depression-born inquiry into the workings of Canada's financial system went to Montreal to get it because the great man felt indisposed. When Governor Graham Towers of the Bank of Canada appeared before a parliamentary committee in 1938, newspapers contrasted his deference with the haughty condescension exhibited by Canada's bankers not so many years earlier on the rare occasions when they discussed the mysteries of their sanctified craft. Canada has never been debunked. Gustavus Myers, who had disinterred American robber barons from their graves in no odor of sanctity, came to Canada from Chicago before the World War to compile a History of Canadian Wealth. He wrote only one volume of it of which the copies extant could be counted almost on the fingers of one's hands. What became of the rest of them and of the second volume which should have followed is not known but a perusal of that part of Mr. Myers's work which did get into print encourages a guess.

Canadians are less impulsive than Americans and far

less given to violence. The gun on the hip has never been part of the Canadian tradition, nor the cure of color blindness by auto-da-fé. Canada has hanged rebels but no "radicals." Nobody has ever tried to assassinate a Canadian Prime Minister, although the Fenians shot down a Canadian statesman of lesser rank in Thomas D'Arcy McGee. Gangsterism is only sporadic in Canada and organized racketeering unknown. No hooded figures have ever dominated the Canadian night scene. The law tolerates fewer technicalities and is far swifter. Relatively fewer Canadians murder each other and many more are hanged when they do.

Justice, if more efficient in Canada, is also more dignified and aloof. Trial by newspaper is not tolerated and he would be a bold man who took a camera and a flashlight bulb into a courtroom. The law of slander is more strictly enforced, as one of Premier Aberhart's Social Credit henchmen discovered when he referred to opponents of that monetary theory as "bankers' toadies" and went to jail for it. Aside from the fact that they are more restricted, the uses of publicity are neither so sweet nor so understood. Canadian like British Prime Ministers are chary of giving interviews and prefer to make announcements, if at all possible, in Parliament. They do not find it necessary to be photographed in cowboy hats, or in bucolic surroundings, or even in the bosom of their families. Although Canada has had many stars in Hollywood none of them went there as "Miss Canada," for the female form, though admired, is not apotheosized.

Canada, like the United States, is Puritanical at heart but it is at the same time more tolerant. The senior Dominion has had two Roman Catholic Prime Ministers: Sir John Thompson, who was an English Catholic, and Sir Wilfrid Laurier, a French Catholic. Although part of Premier Aberhart's appeal to the Alberta prairies was the somewhat apocalyptic Bible teaching he dispensed over the radio, there is less fundamentalism in Canadian Protestantism than in American. Catholicism in Canada, although far more important in point of relative numbers than in the United States, is less of a political power than it would be if its adherents all spoke the same tongue.

The differences that have been cited between Canadians and Americans are differences of tempo rather than of character and reveal themselves in the mass rather than in the individual. The gap that divides the Canadian from the Englishman is far wider, despite the best efforts of the Imperial Daughters of the Empire, the English-Speaking Union, the Loyal Orange Lodges, and the United Empire Loyalist Associations to bridge it. And yet disloyalty in Canada is disloyalty to England and a Canadian study group can report to the 1933 British Commonwealth Relations Conference in Toronto that "the Empire is so great a power for good in the world that it would threaten an incalculable disaster should it be endangered or weakened by our deliberately adopting a policy opposed to that of Great Britain on any major issue."

On the other hand Mr. Maxime Raymond, Liberal member of Parliament for a Quebec constituency, can declare: "Interest guides all nations. Our interest tells us not to participate in any foreign war and consequently not to prepare therefor. Our policy should be essentially a Canadian policy."

9

There Is a French-Canadian Nationality

PROBABLY the most striking thing about Canada, considered either as a British or a North American nation, is that it is one-third French. It is the only country on this continent with two official languages, and French is one of them. Canada's French inhabitants are, except for the Indians, its oldest. Their political record is remarkable. Having colonized Canada, they were conquered by Great Britain. Yet only fifteen years later, when Britain's estranged sons to the south rose in rebellion against her, the French Canadians refused to join them and even helped to rout the armies of Montgomery and Arnold when they attacked Quebec. In 1812 they defeated new American invaders at Lacolle and Châteauguay. It can almost be said that Canada is still British today because she was French.

But though they have helped to keep Canada British, the French Canadians have stayed French. At the same time, paradoxically, they are neither English nor French in their political sympathies or emotional attachments, but purely Canadian. One of the most extraordinary facts about this extraordinarily vital and persistent people, who represent the most important French-speaking community outside of France and who have founded at Montreal the third largest French city in the world, is that—in the words of one of their priest-professors—"French Canadians have no mother country."

They were abandoned by France in 1763 and they have disapproved of the course she has followed since. Long before the Conquest, the French of Canada and of Old France had begun to be two separate peoples. The colonials had been looked down on and neglected when they were not being plundered by such rogues as the rascally Intendant Bigot. The Encyclopedists then rising to fame in France had sneered at the colony which Voltaire described as "a few acres of snow." After the Cession in 1763, these sons and daughters of France who had held out so bravely against snow and cold, the savagery of the Indian, and the hostility of their fellow-colonists of New England, were left to their fate. The Duc de Choiseul, according to Pierre Gaxotte, "was able to boast, without provoking derision, that he had played a fine trick on the English by letting them have Canada."

The colonists, according to Denis-Benjamin Viger, a premier of Lower Canada, "had become the plaything of a military tyranny and of an organized rapacity which amazed even the French ministry when the depths of its iniquity were spread before the eyes of an indignant nation, and notwithstanding the attachment they felt for a motherland which had become an unnatural mother, notwithstanding the ardent and almost indomitable zeal with which they had defended the land step by step, they could not feel that the Conquest was anything but a blessing from Heaven. . . . The complete revolution in all its civil and religious institutions which France had passed through subsequently, the evils from which it has suffered on home soil and in the colonies in spite of the brilliant role it is still playing in international affairs, have but added to that feeling."

The 65,000 French Canadians deserted by their mother country on the shores of the St. Lawrence had no easy time of it for the first ten years of the English Conquest. A royal proclamation in 1764 deprived them of their laws and a test oath made them aliens in their own country. That country still reflected the attentions of the New England Rangers under the famous Major Rogers, who had been ordered by General Wolfe to lay it waste to punish the peasantry for taking up arms in support of General Montcalm. Carpet-baggers flocked into Canada from the English settlements with the laudable intention of plundering it. But fortunately for the French Canadians rebellious murmurings began to be heard in the south. Sir Guy Carleton, third English governor of Canada, urged that the French subjects be well treated to make them immune to the infection. In 1774 the Quebec Act restored French law in civil matters and granted them the free practice of their religion. The wisdom of the concession was shown two years later, when the Continental Congress sent Benjamin Franklin, Samuel Chase, and Carroll of Carrollton to Montreal, accompanied by Father Carroll, a Jesuit and later the first Roman Catholic bishop in the United States. The French Canadians, counseled by their clergy, rejected their advances as they later did those of their own compatriot, Lafayette.

Thirty-six years later they again took up arms in defense

of their country against the United States. The French
Canadians were natural soldiers and they had heroic traditions to inspire them. In 1660 Adam Dollard with sixteen
companions had saved the infant French colony at the cost
of their own lives. In a ruinous log fort at the foot of that
formidable rapid of the Ottawa River known as the Long
Sault, they had held off a thousand Iroquois for eight days.
On the eighth they were murdered to a man, but their
discomfited assailants, amazed at such heroism, abandoned
their design of attacking Montreal. In direct line with this
Thermopylaean exploit was the defeat by 350 French Canadians under the gallant de Salaberry of ten times as many
Americans at the battle of Châteauguay.

New France became Lower Canada. There some French
Canadians, like some English Canadians in Upper Canada,
fought for their liberties in the Rebellion of 1837 against
an overbearing Tory autocracy. Like the Ontario rebels,
their efforts were rewarded first by punishment and then by
self-government. Obtaining self-government, they played
their part worthily in Canadian affairs. Sir George Etienne
Cartier, one of the rebels, became one of the chief architects of Canadian Confederation in 1867. It was largely due
to his influence that the Dominion became a federal rather
than a legislative union.

The younger and more nationalistic French Canadians
fought Confederation. Among them was a young man
named Laurier, who declared that it would be "the tomb
of the French race." He lived to become the first French-
Canadian Prime Minister of the confederated Canada and
one of the greatest figures who ever shaped her destiny. It
was well that he was at the head of affairs during the South

African War, when his compatriots were feeling, and saying, that the war was none of their business and were consequently being attacked in Ontario as "traitors." Trouble
was avoided in 1899 but it came in 1917 during the World
War. At the outbreak of that war Laurier, in an eloquent
speech, had proclaimed his loyalty to the British Crown
under which French Canada had obtained and enjoyed its
liberties. His compatriots had raised in the 22nd Battalion,
the famous "Van Doos," a unit whose record is one of the
most gallant in the history of the Canadian Corps. But
Henri Bourassa, flaming Nationalist and editor of the influential *Le Devoir,* declared that "the peril which threatens all French culture on this continent is not German
militarism; it is Anglo-Saxon commercialism. The insidious
influence which undermines in America Catholic thought
and action is not the philosophy of Nietzsche, but Anglo-
Protestant agnosticism." Anglo-Protestant tactlessness was
to do much harm. Sir Sam Hughes, Canada's energetic but
ill-balanced Minister of Militia, chose to send a Protestant
minister to Quebec as chief recruiting officer. As a result,
recruiting under Canada's then voluntary system practically ceased in French Canada. The Conservative leader,
Sir Robert Borden, formed a union government with the
assistance of English Liberals to put conscription into effect.
Laurier, faced by a harsh choice, fell back upon the bosom
of his own people and emerged from a losing fight at the
polls with 63 out of Quebec's 65 seats and only 20 from the
rest of that Canada which had once hearkened so readily
to his golden voice.

The shadows never lifted again from the career of the
great leader. War hatreds, however, slowly dissipated and

French Canada, whose political instinct has always been too sound to form a distinct "French party" and thus to unite the rest of Canada against it, again divided its allegiance in federal affairs. In provincial politics it made a great change in 1936. The Liberal party which had enjoyed thirty-nine years of unbroken rule left office amid the odor of scandal and was succeeded by the overwhelmingly Conservative "National Union party" under the premiership of Maurice Duplessis. Duplessis was a bachelor, a lawyer, and as a politician a French-Canadian counterpart of Premier Hepburn of Ontario, with whom he soon made common cause against the Liberal Federal Government of Prime Minister Mackenzie King.

To those Canadians who cherished freedom and democratic institutions Maurice Duplessis soon became a sinister figure. Not a few of the phenomena which accompanied or dictated the course of his administration seemed to be after the pattern already set by Fascist Europe. Riots, demonstrations, beatings, the restriction of free speech, discrimination against international trade unionism in favor of a provincial unionism more amenable to direction by the Government and the Catholic Church, the persecution of radicalism side by side with the toleration of blue-shirted Fascism, the censoring of films on religious and national grounds, criticism by the ecclesiastical authorities of the freedom of the press heralding press censorship by padlock, the emergence of a narrow nationalism denouncing "English and American trustards" and Jews, all these things took place in Quebec during the first two years the Duplessis government held office.

It looked as if to the other divisions that threatened

Canada's unity was to be added the experience of finding itself one-quarter padlocked and three-quarters free, as if French Canada were to become a totalitarian province so sharply differentiated from the rest of the country by intent and circumstance as to be virtually a separate state. A Padlock Law whose validity the Federal Government never found it expedient to challenge was framed by Premier Duplessis against "Communism" and applied indiscriminately against radical, liberal, and labor leader. A zealous but uninformed secret police confiscated the works of Mark Twain and Robert Louis Stevenson—sometimes it seemed to be enough if the book were bound in red—under the impression apparently that they might engender what the Japanese police call "dangerous thoughts." This writer, although he had taken a milder view of the import of all this than many of his newspaper colleagues, did not altogether escape its manifestations. Returning to his apartment in Montreal after an absence in Ottawa, he found that it had been ransacked from end to end by searchers who had examined everything but taken nothing. Only one room had been left in order—the workroom, where, if anywhere, secret instructions from the Kremlin might have been expected to repose. And that, alas, was of an orderliness which he had never been able to achieve. Montreal city police who were called in were at first mystified. Then they suddenly lost enthusiasm for the chase. They may have considered it all the work of Snow White and the Seven Dwarfs, whose story was then current on the screen.

In any event it was all very unkind, since the writer had already, in his newspaper correspondence, accepted as sincere the Quebec Government's disavowal of wholehearted

Fascism and proclaimed it French nationalism in a newer and currently fashionable form. French Canadians had complained with justice that they were hewers of wood and drawers of water in their own province. They could hardly hope, he had pointed out, to benefit economically from Fascism. Nor would it be anything but inept to conclude that Premier Duplessis or His Eminence Cardinal Villeneuve desired to serve the interests of alien capitalism for its own sake. It was the nationalistic and authoritarian rather than the economic aspects of Fascism that obviously appealed to them. They saw in them a golden opportunity to keep the Catholic French-Canadian French and Catholic, an ideal lately menaced by "Americanism" and other modern influences.

Critics, contrasting Quebec's new course with that French-Canadian championship of liberty and democracy eloquently expressed by Sir Wilfrid Laurier—"Freedom breeds loyalty: coercion always was the mother of rebellion"—were questioning the sincerity of the motives which inspired it. But a brief glance at her history indicated that though the policy might seem new it was actually rooted deep in the past of French Canada. In turning to authoritarianism she was merely returning to it. No other race on this continent has so absolutist a tradition. The Puritans, ruled though they were by a tyrannical moral code, came to America in search of freedom. Their descendants became political rebels. But the first Canadians came to Canada for the greater glory of a hierarchical church and absolutist king, served him till he failed them, and then served his vanquisher. Their own system was semi-feudal, with authority divided between governor and bishop, and many a wrangle between them marked uncertainty as to what should be rendered unto Caesar.

From 1608 to 1663, its first period of colonization, Canada had actually been a theocratic state, with priests ruling the settlements in the absence of civil power. The Canadian clergy were ultramontane, not Gallican. They believed in the supremacy of the Pope, the complete independence of the Church, and the submission of the state to the Church as far as possible. The famous Bishop Laval, after a series of conflicts with the early governors of the colony, finally named his own governors.

To this day the Church has scarcely relaxed her hold on Quebec. Unity of race and language, the isolated parish life of the farming communities, the religious intolerance of some English Canadians, the heritage of a semi-theocratic structure, all have helped. But the determining factor, perhaps, has been the widespread realization that religion was the only cement that could hold the French-Canadian race together. If what differentiates Jean Baptiste so sharply from the other 155,000,000 odd inhabitants of North America is his way of life, his clergy are guides pointing out that way. It is they who have maintained the ideal of the family as the basis of authority and the source of joy. It is they who have encouraged him to root himself firmly in the soil that no factory roofs may obstruct his view of Heaven. They have taught him to look with a scornful eye on the dollar-chasing activities of his English-speaking compatriots, whose reconciliation of a fervent interest in the material gains of this world with a fervent hope of spiritual rewards in the next excites his derision.

Little in French Canada to this day is done without the

Church and nothing can flourish against it. Education in Quebec is entirely under its control. There are twenty-five different religious communities and orders which engage in education, agriculture, charity work, hospital service, and missionary efforts. A single church in Montreal has its own schools, guilds for boys, men, women, and young girls, sewing circles, a mothers' help organization, three homes for young women, a temperance society, and several different organizations whose object is to help the poor. There are a dozen leagues and associations, such as the Young Catholic Workmen or the Young Patriots, by which French-Canadian youth of all ages are kept in close touch with the Church. To incur the displeasure of the Church would be, for the politician or professional man in French Canada, a heavy and perhaps fatal handicap. Sir Wilfrid Laurier, in his early days, fought the Quebec hierarchy and won. But he had the assistance of the Vatican and there are few Lauriers. The part played by the Church in politics is far less obvious and direct now than it was in earlier times, when the bishops sometimes went so far as to declare, as did Bishop Bourget of Montreal, that "no Catholic is allowed to proclaim himself a moderate Liberal" and Rome itself requested them to desist. But its influence, which is always on the side of conservatism, is still great.

A tight hand is also kept by the Catholic clergy on the morals of their flock. This, like so much in Quebec, derives from early usage. The manners of New France were ruled as rigidly by its priests as those of the Puritans farther south. Bishop Laval was America's first prohibitionist. His successor, Bishop Saint Vallier, enjoined Governor Denonville not to countenance balls or dances, warned the

Governor's daughter against the wearing of "immodest curls so expressly forbidden in the epistles of St. Peter and St. Paul," conceded that in view of her youth she might indulge in a little moderate dancing "provided it is solely with persons of her own sex and in the presence of madame her mother." "One can neither go on a pleasure party, nor play a game of cards, nor visit the ladies," complained that malicious young chronicler of the manners and customs of the colony, La Hontan, "without the curé knowing it and preaching about it publicly from his pulpit."

The youth of French Canada allows itself more latitude now, especially in the cities, but country curés in recent times have been known to break up country dances with a horsewhip. The Government, influenced by the Church, is also at pains to safeguard the morals of its people. Quebec city police not long ago confiscated as "dirty literature" copies of five American magazines, including *Look* and *Coronet*. The film *Emile Zola* was banned, Zola's works being on the Index Expurgatorius, and from time to time films of lesser merit share the same fate. Cardinal Villeneuve has protested against that freedom of the press which gave newspapers a "license to teach all error, peddle all calumny."

Just as the Church in Quebec has been untouched by Gallicanism, the French Canadian has been a Frenchman without benefit of Montesquieu, Voltaire, Descartes, Rousseau, or the French Revolution. His mind is still shaped on seventeenth-century lines. In his universities he is taught to admire Corneille, Racine, Bossuet, and Fénelon above modern writers. If he reads Voltaire, Rousseau, and Hugo it is not with the approval of the seminary. He is encouraged toward a classical rather than a scientific education.

As a people French Canadians have proved good mixed farmers, magnificent pioneers, gifted politicians, doctors, and lawyers. They write and speak with more felicity than English Canadians but their orators, like their writers, have been noted more for perfection of form than for originality of content. They are shrewd traders but have supplied artisans and craftsmen to industry rather than executives, owners, or entrepreneurs. Their banking, insurance, and investment are done in large part with English companies. Their minor share in the industry, commerce, and finance of their own province is one of their complaints against the English Canadian. They account for it largely by the lack of that capital which for fifty years flowed from London to English Canadian banks and enterprises. It does not seem a sufficient reason. The commercial potentialities of French-Canadian clannishness would appear to be considerable and so would that complete legislative control enjoyed for three-quarters of a century over Quebec province. Since the Old Country Frenchman has shown neither disinclination nor inability to manage his own industrial and financial affairs, the mediocre performance of his Canadian cousin in these fields must be ascribed largely to his education, which does not fit him for them, and his philosophy of living, which values other successes more highly.

The French Canadian is vivacious but solid, lighthearted but religious, thrifty but not accumulative. He has an acute sense of family, respect for law, and reverence for tradition. A folklore haunted by witches and werewolves and what has been described as the best collection of folksongs in the world link with his New and Old World past a culture unique on this continent. His literature has looked backward and his whole outlook on life has been permeated by a desire to "lie at anchor in the stream of time." To Goldwin Smith he was a relic of the past "preserved like a Siberian mammoth in ice." His culture has been more recently and fairly described as "an extraordinary structure of racialism, religion, piety, scholasticism, paternalism, and authoritarianism, a simple peasant life, a golden age of urbane though old-fashioned culture, of priestly predominance, domestic propriety, and large families."

Of late years that golden age has been threatened by modernism and that simple peasant life has been giving way to industrialization and urbanization. The peasant is being transformed into a proletarian. In the city he is farther from the paternal eye of his priest and accessible to "Americanization" via the radio, film, newspaper, and magazine, trade union or office contacts. Quebec actually has less than its proportionate share of Canadian Communism but there, as elsewhere, economic discontent has provided a ferment for new and frothy ideas. Still more alarming, it has put a question-mark before the Catholic policy and the French-Canadian practice of fecundity. When it did that it threatened to blunt the chief instrument of French Canada's persistence, its high survival rate.

For the 65,000 French Canadians who became British in 1763 have grown to at least 3,500,000 in 1940. They were just under 3,000,000 in 1931, when the last census was taken, and must be nearly a third of Canada's population today, since in the intervening period they have lost little or nothing by emigration. They have overflowed into East-

ern Ontario, risen from 16 per cent in the Maritime Provinces to 33 per cent, and in New Brunswick close to equality. Their survival rate, or excess of births over deaths,
today is 15 per 1000 compared with 7.6 in the largely English province of Ontario and 4.7 in the wholly English
province of British Columbia. Their priests have encouraged early marriage and anathematized birth control. Even
in Eastern Ontario this spirit a few years ago inspired the
prosecution of an English-Canadian woman who had distributed contraceptives among French Canadians.

But even without priestly prescription the French
Canadian would probably be fruitful, since large families
were encouraged by subsidy in the seventeenth century
from which he derives his traditions. Louis XIV paid a
pension of 400 livres to the head of a family of twelve,
and Colbert, his minister, offered 1200 to those who had
fifteen children. Louis had also ordered that "preference
should always be extended, when a distribution of honors
or patronage takes place, to men with large progeny around
them," while an order had been issued forbidding the unhappy bachelor to "hunt, fish, trade with the Indians, or
go into the woods under any pretense whatsoever." To
enable the bachelor to escape such punishments a thousand young women were sent out from France in eight
years to find husbands. They were known as "the King's
girls" and, according to the frivolous La Hontan, "the
plumpest were taken first, because it was thought being
less active they were more likely to stay at home and could
resist the winter cold better."

Louis XIV was generally at war and could not spare
men for the new colony. It had to depend for growth on

its own natural increase. It is under the same necessity today and so well has it mastered its task that in another fifty years, unless English-speaking Canada receives accessions through immigration, it will be outnumbered by French Canada. What if this unrestricted fruitfulness enjoins sacrifice and a lower standard of living! Blessed are the meek, for they shall inherit the earth. So Church and Government strive to keep their folk upon the land, where large families may find their own living. Far up in Northern Quebec, where Americanizing influences do not penetrate, they have thrown open land for colonization. No settler of radical opinions, economic or religious, need apply. For the French Canadian who does drift to the city and its factories the Church has organized and the government encouraged the National Catholic Syndicates. Each is under the watchful eye of a chaplain, who in practice sometimes acts as business director as well as moral guide. Already the Syndicates claim to have 45,000 members and they are growing fast.

What his leaders aspire to for the French Canadian, if he will but remain true to his race and religion, is not only transfiguration in the next world but dominion in this, not only happiness in the hereafter as the crown of a fruitful life but the land of Canada and the fullness thereof as the prize of a fruitful race. In the attainment of that goal democratic forms will be used if they seem to be the best means of safeguarding French autonomy but if not, as recent experience has indicated, a more authoritative system will be substituted for them.

Currently democracy seems to be in for a new lease of life. Mr. Duplessis is out of office and Mr. Adelard Godbout, a Liberal who attacked his highhanded methods while in opposition, has succeeded him. The result was due principally to Mr. Ernest Lapointe. Canada kept one French-Canadian Prime Minister in office for fifteen years. It might have found another in Ernest Lapointe had his courage and capacity been leavened with less loyalty to Mr. Mackenzie King and fired by more ambition. Never did he prove his qualities better than in the provincial general election called by Premier Duplessis at the beginning of the war, ostensibly to protest against infringement of Quebec's rights by the emergency measures of the Federal Government.

Mr. Lapointe announced that if Mr. Duplessis were re-elected he and the other three Quebec members of the federal cabinet would accept it as a vote against the Government's war measures and resign. He was urged, even by Conservative newspaper editors, not to take the situation so seriously. They pointed out that Duplessis was making use of the war merely as an election device. He was certain to be re-elected, but his lack of scruple should not be allowed to array the other eight provinces of Canada against Quebec in a federal general election, which would be the inevitable result of the resignation of four ministers from Mr. King's cabinet. But Mr. Lapointe persisted and risked not only his own office but the prestige of the Federal Government by throwing himself heart and soul into the provincial campaign. The event proved that he had been not only courageous but also far-seeing. Ernest Lapointe is a Liberal in the true tradition of Laurier.

Thanks to its native vitality and the efforts of church and state, French Canada today represents one of history's miracles. The handful left to the mercies of an alien conqueror by their mother country almost two hundred years ago have been sundered from it ever since. Yet they have survived into this modern day not only with race, religion, and way of living intact but with numbers so increased that they threaten to swamp their conquerors. In Europe a minority means an *irredenta,* constantly nourishing from the parent source its hopes, its traditions, and its prejudices. But there has been no *irredenta* in Canada. France ceded it in 1763. Not until 1855 did the French frigate *La Capricieuse* sail up the St. Lawrence to Quebec to renew the contact broken so long ago. When the British Foreign Office took exception to some of the speeches made by its commander, even this mild demonstration of paternal interest was not renewed for many years. France, to all appearances, remained indifferent to the fate of her former children. The children, in turn, have disapproved of their free-living, free-thinking, anticlerical, and republican mother.

And yet Old France should be proud of French Canada. Biologically its people are superior, since the family of Jean Baptiste is ever growing while that of Marianne declines. Racially these emigrants from Normandy have shown themselves more persistent even than those other Normans who conquered England in 1066. For the descendants of William the Conqueror were themselves conquered by time, leaving behind them only a chapter in the history of the Anglo-Saxon, a leaven of Latin in the English language, and a trace of blue in the English blood. But the French, who were first in Canada, are still in Canada and still French. When they marry their English-speaking compatriots it is to absorb them. Many a traveler in the country of the St. Lawrence has been disconcerted on challenging an O'Flaherty or a McTavish in English to find that he spoke only French.

The French Canadians are a vigorous, persistent, and rapidly increasing minority. Because they are a minority and particularly because they are a more assimilating than assimilable one, they are resented by their English-speaking fellow-citizens. They return this resentment. The situation being what it is, this result is unavoidable. As a minority, French Canadians feel an irking sense of inferiority. As the colonizers of the country and the more vital race biologically, they feel superior. As a people whose whole hopes are centered in Canada and complicated by no transatlantic cross-loyalties, they can neither understand nor approve the inability of their English-speaking compatriots to be satisfied merely with being Canadian.

Their principal grievance is that they do not enjoy in the rest of Canada the same privileges as in Quebec. French is an official language. But education is a provincial matter and since there is an English-speaking majority in eight of Canada's nine provinces the children of French minorities in most of them must receive instruction largely in English. What the French Canadians desire is the establishment of French-speaking separate schools but so far neither the provincial educational authorities nor their Irish fellow-Catholics have proved very co-operative.

That is why Cardinal Villeneuve, in an address in 1939 before the National Press Club in Washington, referred to the "grudging" manner in which French Canada was accorded its rights. His Eminence could not have been thinking of Quebec, where the French Canadian reigns supreme. He has been allowed there to enact in the Padlock Law legislation which wounds at least the spirit of Canadian criminal law. His judges increasingly tend to substitute the canon law of the Catholic Church for the civil law governing marriages. "Mixed marriages" between Protestants and Catholics are regularly held invalid by certain Quebec judges unless celebrated by a Catholic priest. They have persisted in rendering such judgments although the highest Canadian court of appeal has pronounced against the contention on which they are founded.

Any considerable strengthening of Canada's English population caused by immigration as after German bombing in a long war would be regarded with dismay by those leaders of French Canada who have nourished hopes of early equality and eventual domination. They would interpret it not only as dooming them to perpetual numerical inferiority but as committing their country to perpetual participation in costly imperial adventures. The creation of a separate French state on the St. Lawrence, hitherto advocated only by a minority, might commend itself in such circumstances as a last resort. It has never yet been encouraged by the political or ecclesiastical leaders of Quebec, since the creation of a French enclave would doom the 500,000 French Canadians who live in other parts of Canada to assimilation and end their own dream of predominating throughout the whole Dominion and not merely a part of it.

That dream, in the opinion of detached observers, will never be realized. André Siegfried, Old Country Frenchman whose study of French Canada is a standard work, predicts that the English Canadians would revolt before they saw themselves outvoted. They might even prefer annexation by the United States and the United States has always assimilated her white minorities. A less drastic solution would be the resumption of immigration. Frenchmen do not emigrate—although a million French Canadians have emigrated to the United States—and it has been demonstrated that other European newcomers to Canada adopt British speech and customs rather than French ones.

10

Canadian Parties and Politics

CANADA'S political institutions and political parties, like nearly everything else Canadian, are a British-American amalgam. Her municipal administration is far more American than English. But her government is the British parliamentary system adapted to federalism. Like the United States but unlike England, Canada has a written constitution. But it merely demarcates the respective jurisdictions of the Dominion and the provinces and does not limit governmental authority over the citizen. It does not define a social ideal such as that all men are created free and equal. It is a piece of political machinery, a statute rather than a constitution.

If her constitution has laid down for Canada the basis of no social creed, neither has she ever had a Hamilton or Jefferson to furnish her parties with a choice of political philosophies. Though the Rebellion of 1837 was the decisive event which brought her responsible government, her leaders prefer to forget rather than to glorify it. At the back of Canada's political mind is neither a revolution nor a Bill of Rights. There is a belief in responsible government and representative institutions, inherited from Great Britain, modified in Quebec by a paternalistic tradition and sometimes in the prairie West by a willingness imported from the United States to experiment with those devices of a more direct democracy, the referendum and the recall.

Since she had a horrible example of the results of its refusal next door, Canada was the first British colony to get self-government. But even Canada did not obtain it without rebelling, since the first idea of the British Government was that the American Revolution would not have taken place if a tighter hand had been kept on the Thirteen Colonies. But when the theory did not work the Government quickly recognized, and repaired, its mistake. Canada was the first to reconcile local autonomy with membership of an Empire, the touchstone of Britain's ability to avoid another American Revolution, the laboratory in which was worked out the formula for "the third British Empire."

After the rebellion in Upper and Lower Canada—Quebec and Ontario—had been suppressed, the British Government sent out Lord Durham to act as governor-general and high commissioner with the duty of determining what the trouble was and how it could be remedied. Lord Durham, an English Liberal politician of high talent, became the author of responsible government in Canada and if not the father at least the grandfather of Confederation. But to the Canadians who viewed his coming he must have seemed strangely cast for the part. He arrived invested with arbitrary powers and clothed in the prestige of a distinguished career. He entered Quebec sitting haughtily astride a white charger and followed by a cortege that suggested an eastern despot rather than a western liberator. But he soon demonstrated that he meant to carry out his pledge "to know nothing of a British, a French, or a Canadian party but to look on them all alike as Her Majesty's subjects." His report is the most searching, eloquent, and valuable pronouncement on colonial policy in the English language. He informed London that he found it impossible "to understand how any English statesmen could ever have imagined that representative and irresponsible government could be successfully combined. . . . To suppose that such a system would work well there, implied a belief that the French Canadians have enjoyed representative institutions for half a century without acquiring any of the characteristics of a free people; that Englishmen renounce every political opinion and feeling when they enter a colony, or that the spirit of Anglo-Saxon freedom is utterly changed and weakened among those who are transplanted across the Atlantic."

Memorable words which, if uttered sixty-three years earlier, might have changed the whole destiny of the United States. They became a charter for Canada. Though the imperial authorities made it quite obvious that they did not see how a governor responsible to the British Government could act on the advice of ministers responsible to a colonial legislature, Lord John Russell, then British Colonial Secretary, declared that Queen Victoria "had no desire to maintain any system of policy among her North American subjects which opinion condemns." Some early governors of Canada found it difficult to understand or approve the new dispensation. Lord Metcalfe, who was brought from India to assume the post, brought some of his Indian ideas with him. His idea of responsible government was that the governor should bend it to the will of the Crown and use all the prestige and if necessary the authority of his office to do so. The first result of these convictions was to bring about the resignation of the government which under the leadership of Robert Baldwin, the Reform leader of English-speaking Upper Canada, and Mr. Louis Hippolyte Lafontaine, a great French Canadian, had worked patiently and effectively to restore harmony after the revolution. Fortunately Lord Metcalfe was soon followed by Lord Elgin, who was Lord Durham's son-in-law and had some of the statesman-like gifts of that administrator. Lord Elgin left responsible government so surely based in Canada that it was never subsequently endangered.

In the maritime provinces of New Brunswick and Nova Scotia, then separate colonies, there was a parallel history of struggles between legislative assemblies and early governors. It was enlivened in Nova Scotia by the personal dispute between Lord Falkland and Joseph Howe, the son of a Loyalist printer from Boston who became one of the fathers of Confederation and a great Canadian statesman. Lord Falkland, before he became governor-general, had been a lord of the bedchamber and husband of a daughter of William IV. This great personage tried to detach the Liberal party of Nova Scotia from Howe's leadership and to this end attacked him in dispatches to the Colonial Office. When the Colonial Office supported his attitude he disclosed the correspondence so that it could be employed as campaign material against the Liberals. Finally Howe declared to a disorderly Assembly that if "the infamous system" of libeling respectable colonists in dispatches to the Colonial Office were continued "without their having any means of redress . . . some colonist will by-and-by, or I am much mistaken, hire a black fellow to horsewhip a lieutenant-governor." Fortunately, before this one-man revolution could take place Lord Falkland was transferred to Bombay, a more congenial field for an administrator with his ideas.

Having obtained a government responsible to the people, Canadians gradually assumed control over their domestic and foreign affairs. In 1846 they were authorized to make their own tariffs, although not until 1923 did Canada negotiate and sign her own treaties. In 1926 she sent her own minister to Washington. Now she has ministers also in Tokyo, Paris, Brussels, and The Hague.

In 1867 the two Canadas, Nova Scotia, and New Brunswick bound themselves together by the statesman-like act of Confederation, thus forming the nucleus of a dominion to which British Columbia was admitted in 1871 and Prince Edward Island in 1873. The British North America Act, which constituted the confederacy, gave her a system of government thoroughly English, with no division between the executive and legislative functions, no contrivance of checks and balances. That partial decentralization of power known as federalism, of which Canada was the first exponent in the British Empire, was derived from the United States. But the Fathers of Confederation fondly imagined that they had not only imitated the example of their next-door neighbor but improved upon it. Sir John A. Macdonald, like Alexander Hamilton, believed in a strong central government and managed to a greater extent than Hamilton to embody his ideas in the British North America Act. He gave the Federal Government, in addition to the powers of the American Federal Government, control over marriage, divorce, and criminal law, including the appointment of judges, the right to nominate and remove the provincial lieutenant-governors, and the important power of veto over provincial legislation. Finally he thought he had arranged for the grant to the Federal Government of all power not expressly given to the provinces. In the United States it was different but Macdonald believed that Canada had avoided "the defects which time and events have shown to exist in the American constitution." He declared afterwards that in framing the British North America Act Canada "had the advantage of the experience of the United States. . . . I think and believe that it is one of the most perfect organizations that ever governed a free people."

Seldom has the fallibility of human hopes been better demonstrated. Like many another will, this bequest of all political wisdom has been successfully attacked in the courts. The powers of the central government have been whittled down until not it, but the provinces, have become residuary legatees. Whereas the United States Supreme Court has interpreted the American constitution to widen the powers of the central government the British Privy Council, by a series of remarkable decisions, has clipped the wings of the Canadian Federal Government. A far-fetched interpretation of the clause of the British North America Act giving the provinces jurisdiction over "property and civil rights" has transferred to them the residuum of power intended for the Dominion. For instance, in 1923 the Privy Council held that the Industrial Disputes Investigation Act, which authorized the Federal Labor

Minister to appoint conciliating and investigating boards to avert strikes and lockouts, was intervention in a matter affecting "property and civil rights." Overruling the Canadian Supreme Court, the Law Lords declared the residuary power of the Dominion Parliament to make laws "for the peace, order, and good government of Canada" was only an emergency power.

The decision of the Privy Council has hamstrung the central government in its attempts to provide uniform machinery for conciliating industrial disputes, putting a ceiling on hours and a floor under wages, establishing unemployment insurance, and formulating corporation law. But it has imposed an even more serious disability which promises to handicap Canada in her external relations. It has robbed her Federal Government of that "all-comprehensive" power to control foreign relations possessed by the Federal Government of the United States. The British North America Act declared that the Canadian Parliament should be endowed with all the powers "for performing the obligations of Canada or any province thereof as part of the British Empire, towards foreign countries, arising under treaties between the Empire and such foreign countries." This was believed until recently to mean that the Canadian Federal Government had power to override provincial jurisdiction in order to discharge the treaty obligations of Canada as part of the Empire, even if the treaty applied only to Canada and not to the whole Empire. Acting on this understanding, Canada invaded provincial jurisdiction to make such pacts as the Boundary Waters Treaty of 1909. The Boundary Waters Treaty was not only a notable achievement in international arbitration but a great step forward in Canada's attainment of diplomatic status. No instrument has proved more useful to Canadian-American relations.

But when Mr. R. B. Bennett tried to make use of draft conventions of the International Labor Organization to put through an eight-hour day and establish minimum-wage machinery as part of his New Deal, the Privy Council declared the legislation *ultra vires.* It denied that the British North America Act had conferred any overriding legislative power on the Canadian Parliament except possibly in the case of treaties that affected the whole British Empire. It declared that the obligation to implement the International Labor conventions to which it had adhered was not an obligation of Canada as part of the British Empire but "of Canada by virtue of her new status as an international person." That new status had been conferred by the Statute of Westminster, which was supposed to endow Canada with full autonomy. But the decision of the Privy Council indicated that the statute had bereft her of the treaty-making powers she had possessed under the British North America Act in her former subordinate capacity. The effect of it is to endow every Canadian province with a right of veto over the treaty-making power of the Dominion where provincial jurisdiction is affected, and provincial jurisdiction, as a result of judicial interpretation of the vague language of the "property and civil rights" clause, could be stretched to include most subjects. It is highly unlikely, for instance, that the Boundary Waters Treaty could have been concluded a few years ago, when Messrs. Hepburn and Duplessis were fighting every act of the King government.

Why the Privy Council has steadily weakened the central power in Canada and strengthened that of the provinces has been a matter of debate. The most charitable explanation has been that the Law Lords did not understand federalism. The most critical has been that their decisions were influenced by political rather than judicial motives, that these members of Britain's hereditary upper chamber were pursuing a policy employed with success in other parts of the British Empire, that of "divide and rule." Whatever the intention, the result has been to create a strong movement in Canada to substitute the Canadian Supreme Court for the Privy Council as the highest tribunal.

By the Statute of Westminster passed in 1931 by the British Parliament the United Kingdom and the dominions were declared to be "autonomous communities within the British Empire, equal in status, in no way subordinate one to another in any aspect of their domestic or external affairs though united by a common allegiance to the Crown and freely associated as members of the British Commonwealth of Nations." According to Professor William Bennett Munro this embodied almost verbatim "the dicta of Jefferson, Adams, Franklin, Madison, and Wilson as set forth in the writings of these American fathers more than a century ago. Jefferson regarded the British King as the common sovereign, the central link connecting the several portions of the Empire." Franklin had written that "America is not part of the Dominions of England but of the King's Dominions."

Sir John Macdonald had wanted to call the Confederation of which he was the principal architect the "Kingdom of Canada." The British Government vetoed the suggestion for fear of offending anti-monarchists in the United States, whose views had found expression in a resolution by the State of Maine that "any attempt on the part of the Imperial Government of Great Britain to establish monarchical government in North America or to place a viceroyalty by act of Parliament over her several North American provinces, would be an implied infraction of those principles of government which the nation has assumed to maintain upon this continent." But Canada, to all intents and purposes, is a kingdom today. The Governor-General should be called a viceroy, since he now represents the King and not the British Parliament. He drives like a King to the Parliament Buildings, preceded by an escort and hailed by a royal salute, to seat himself there upon a throne and declare in ancient Norman French that *"le roy y veult"* (the King wills it).

When King George VI visited the Canadian Senate Chamber to give royal assent to a number of bills in 1939 his action fitted quite naturally into Canadian procedure. Though she is so American Canada in some ways is the most British of the dominions. Her lower chamber is called a House of Commons as in England, not a House of Representatives as in Australia or a House of Assembly as in South Africa. Since its Senators are appointed for life and a property qualification is demanded of them, Canada's upper chamber resembles the House of Lords more closely than does Australia's, to which Senators are elected for six years. Like the House of Lords, the Canadian Senate represents conservatism, not to say reaction.

Those of its members who are not full of years are full of dollars.

Her provincial legislatures are modeled on the lines of the Federal Parliament except that only Quebec's is bicameral. In her municipal government, city councils divide power with boards of control or other more or less independent administrative bodies. In this, as in their election of mayors by direct vote, Canadians follow an American example, for New York set the pattern for boards of control sixty years ago with its Board of Estimate and Apportionment. Like the United States, too, Canada has separate boards of education and police commissioners. Her civic politics have been marred by far fewer scandals than those which proclaimed in the United States "the shame of the cities." The Canadian is happier in his judicial and police systems. The fact that criminal law is exclusively within federal jurisdiction has been an advantage that Mr. Edgar Hoover would be quick to admit. In the belief that "if you want representation elect, if you want efficiency appoint" the whole judiciary, including crown attorneyships, has been divorced from politics. Since all courts are King's courts, Canada avoids the complications of a dual judicature.

For fifty years after Confederation Canada had only two parties, Liberal and Conservative. During most of the half-century in which they played the game of ins and outs, they might have exchanged names as freely as they exchanged office, since the Liberals were never very liberal nor the Conservatives very conservative. Sir John

Macdonald, Sir Robert Borden, and Mr. R. B. Bennett, changed far more than they conserved. Mr. Mackenzie King, present leader of the Liberal party, is far more of a reactionary.

There was a time in Canada—it seems long ago—when the Liberals stood for free trade and provincial rights and the Conservatives for a national policy of high protection and centralism. The distinction has largely disappeared, though Mr. R. B. Bennett restored it for a few years by raising Canada's tariff wall and seeking to recapture federal authority for the purposes of his New Deal. Since the Conservatives could not do without the western farmers nor the Liberals without the eastern manufacturers both parties had to compromise as Democrats and Republicans have compromised in the United States. The Liberals on the whole have been more friendly to the United States and less ready to participate in imperial councils. The Conservatives under Borden and Meighen were willing to discuss imperial policy and under R. B. Bennett even to determine it. Both parties have championed Canadian autonomy though they had different ideas as to what Canada was to do with her independence when she got it.

Neither has ever been a party of the masses. They have never felt that they could afford it. Elections in Canada are not won by prayers and the corporations from which the parties have derived their campaign funds do not contribute in the spirit in which one gives to a church collection. In the old days they put in their money and took out their concession. Nowadays the transaction is less specific although when the Beauharnois Power Corporation paid $700,000 into the Liberal campaign fund before the 1930

elections it was generally believed that it was not altogether for the sake of Mr. Mackenzie King's beautiful
eyes.

One of the anomalies of Canadian politics is that Quebec, which is essentially conservative, has for the past half-
century given from 50 to 100 per cent of its seats to the
Liberal party. It has thus become for the Liberals in
Canada the equivalent of the "solid South" to the Democrats in the United States. For twenty years after Confederation it was the Conservatives who could rely on a
majority in Quebec. It was Sir Wilfrid Laurier who
brought his countrymen into the Liberal vineyard and it
was resentment of conscription that kept them there from
1917 to 1930. Mr. Mackenzie King has retained Quebec
because he opposed conscription in 1917, has pledged himself against it in the present war, and has commanded the
loyalty of Mr. Ernest Lapointe. But to keep Quebec he
has had to be more conservative than liberal in his policies.

Radicalism, refused a home by the Conservative party
when Mr. R. B. Bennett tried to introduce it as a paying
guest, and denied a place in Liberalism by Mr. King's
temperament and his dependence on Quebec, has found
vehicles in Canada in a succession of "protest" parties.
The Grange, the Patrons' Movement, and the Society of
Equity successively spread across the border from the
United States and sowed in Canada a seed which flowered
into provincial and federal farmers' parties. A Farmers'
government had a brief career in Ontario from 1919 to
1923. In 1921 the United Farmers attained office in Alberta and held it until ousted by an administration proffer-
ing the headier brew of Social Credit. A Progressive party

was elected in Manitoba in 1922 and is still there although it now calls itself Liberal-Progressive.

In the federal field the Progressives flattered but to deceive. In 1921 they were returned second only to the Liberals. But party discipline was weak, the interests of Ontario farmers were not those of prairie wheat-growers, and their leaders could not agree whether to form a national party with the inclusion of other groups or remain an agrarian group. In a decade the party had disintegrated, most of its strength going to the Liberals, some of it to that coalition of Farmer, Labor, and Fabian Socialist elements which handicaps itself with the name of Co-operative Commonwealth Federation and which the public with sounder instinct calls the CCF.

The CCF has done yeoman service in the Federal Parliament and has gained some ground in the provinces. But even its Fabian Socialism does not go down very well with the western farmers, who think of themselves as capitalists even though post-depression statistics have appeared to indicate that they are the rather poorly paid hired men of the banks and mortgage companies. Neither has the CCF received much support from organized labor, whose part in Canadian politics has been negligible as compared with that in Great Britain, Australia, or New Zealand. This is due in Quebec partly to the influence of the Catholic Syndicates and elsewhere to the influence of the American Federation of Labor, with which so many Canadian labor unions are affiliated.

A difficulty with which third parties in Canada have had to contend is that under direct voting in single-member constituencies large minorities may go unrepresented.

In 1935 the fugitive "Reconstruction" party headed by Mr. H. H. Stevens polled almost 10 per cent of the total vote but elected only Mr. Stevens himself. This may have been one of the factors which influenced Mr. Stevens's return to the Conservative fold whence he had departed. The Liberal party, which obtained only 47 per cent of the total vote, got 70 per cent of the seats. In 1896, for that matter, it came to power with a majority of 30 although it had 11,000 fewer votes than the Conservatives. Such results negate democracy. But neither of the two senior parties has ever been willing to adopt proportional representation, the alternative vote, or any other device which would produce a more representative parliament. The argument is that it would lead to group government.

As a matter of fact Canada, like any other sectional country, has group government now. The difference is that the groups play their part in the political caucus and behind the closed doors of the cabinet chamber rather than in the open. Even geographical constituencies cannot save Canada from sectionalism. Nature has divided her into four distinct regions and economic development has reinforced the divisions. Fate has provided her with two races and two religions. A political party must consider all these factors when framing its platform. That is why a Canadian political platform must be broad even though fragile and the advance declarations of party leaders have all the reliability and comprehensiveness of a patent-medicine advertisement. Once elected, a leader must take Canada's regionalism into account not only in all his policies but in all his appointments. In choosing his cabinet, in selecting new senators, he must see that not only the

French in Quebec are represented but the French in New Brunswick, not only the Catholics in Quebec but the Protestants, not only Ontario's Orangemen but its Catholic Irish, Canada's western farmers and Canada's eastern manufacturers.

When it comes to electing a House of Commons sectionalism becomes parochialism. Some of the most useful elements go unrepresented. Few of Canada's intellectuals get into the House of Commons, although Mackenzie King appointed Professor Norman Rogers as his Minister of Labor and then of National Defense. This is unfortunate when foreign affairs are under review. Canada's professors have almost a monopoly of knowledge of the subject but they are outside Parliament. Inside Parliament it is debated on a much lower intellectual level when it is debated at all. The best contributions have been made by the CCF, which has generally numbered in its thin ranks a percentage of English-born Socialists capable of the intellectual rather than the demagogic approach. Some of the French-Canadian contingent, from their own point of view, speak eloquently and well. But it is a pity that Canada has not that separate representation for the universities that obtains in Great Britain.

A similar poverty of ideas is exhibited when broad economic issues are under review. Twenty-five years ago debates were more pointed and more piquant than they are today. That was before circumstances had begun to challenge, and men to doubt, the system under which they lived. Making due allowance for partisanship, they spoke as they thought. But there is a significant, one could almost say a fatal, difference between their thinking today—

as indicated by the reading matter they obtain from the Canadian Parliamentary Library or their conversation in private—and their public speaking. That is why of late years a debate on some such general subject as the address in reply to the Speech from the Throne has produced an impression of utter unreality to the listener with any knowledge of what was going on in the country and in the minds of its citizens. The atmosphere in the Commons chamber seemed often to be not merely cloistered but petrified. At a time when the public mind was full of the fear of war, the sense of economic insecurity, and an uneasy apprehension of the passing of old folkways, the mouths of Canadian members of Parliament were full of complaints about postmasters, wrangles over House rules, and such profound generalities as that more business was needed in government and less government in business. Perhaps the Canadian Parliament has been suffering only from the general malady of democracy, but debate in the Congress of the United States or the Parliament of Great Britain has at least seemed more representative of public thinking and more aware of the fundamental issue.

Canada has had a Socialist party in Parliament for the past ten years, whereas in the United States the disciples of Mr. Norman Thomas are not in Congress. Canada has, at the time of writing, the only Social Credit parliamentary party and certainly the only Social Credit provincial government in the world. Since there is no protection of contract in the Canadian constitution it would be theoretically possible for a radical party to confiscate wealth without due process of law and since a Canadian parliament can delegate all legislative power, there would be little to prevent the administration of Canada by individuals or boards. Canadians, without the benefit of a New Deal, have furnished striking examples of collectivism such as the Ontario Hydro-Electric Commission and the western wheat pools and have done a good deal of planning because they had to plan to stay British. But despite these things Canada is far more conservative than Australia or New Zealand or the United States.

In Canada no Securities and Exchange Commission regulates finance, although what was known as the Price Spreads Inquiry in 1934 indicated there was as much need for it. It has no Federal Trade Commission keeping trade practices fair and advertising veracious, no National Labor Relations Board to enforce collective bargaining or Social Security Board to provide unemployment insurance, no Reconstruction Finance Corporation or Export-Import Bank to supply capital, no WPA to provide work. Canada has a publicly owned railroad system to compete with the privately owned Canadian Pacific Railway, a publicly owned Transcanada air service; it has bonuses and fixed wheat prices for the farmer, a publicly owned central bank instead of a privately owned Federal Reserve System, and a publicly owned Canadian Broadcasting Corporation controlling and competing with private radio stations.

But the railroad system is publicly owned because the Government came to the relief of private investors in the Canadian Northern and Grand Trunk railroads, who, having with official encouragement provided the country with twice as much mileage as she needed, were able to force it to bear most of the loss. The western farmer is being bonused for the same reason as the American and

British farmer, because farming is necessary but for the time being does not pay. The Bank of Canada was nationalized largely to appease monetary reformers within the Liberal party. But Mr. Graham Towers, its capable forty-three-year-old governor, is probably more orthodox in his banking views than Mr. Marriner Eccles, who directs the destinies of the Federal Reserve. The Canadian Broadcasting Corporation is government-owned because it is primarily a device for achieving Canadian unity and preventing the complete Americanization of the Canadian ear.

There is also Mr. Aberhart and his Social Credit government in Alberta. The advent to power in that prairie province of a government headed by an evangelist economist and committed to a policy which might be described as a Townsend dividend grafted on the purchasing-power theories of the Scottish engineer-economist, Major C. H. Douglas, seemed an ominous event at the time to Canadian financiers and politicians. But Mr. Aberhart has turned out to be no more ominous than William Jennings Bryan, whom, in all but oratorical power, he much resembles. A series of adverse court decisions and federal disallowances ended his hope of establishing a monetary Utopia in a single province and excused him from his pledge to pay every citizen of Alberta a monthly dividend. A series of wrangles with Major Douglas proclaimed him a heretic even from the somewhat vague tenets of the Social Credit creed. So Mr. Aberhart, who has not been a bad administrator, remains significant chiefly as the leader of a protest movement. He will be memorable as the first man in Canadian history to combine apocalyptic religion with monetics and to broadcast it over the air waves in the form of a political campaign. Mr. Aberhart is large and pale and flabby, and his manner is as heavy as his figure. But since he could see visions and make his followers see them he is obviously a phenomenon of the mass mind well worth the study of psychologists and politicians, even though Social Credit may prove as transitory in its appeal as was Free Silver south of the border.

11

Is Canada a Failure?

CANADIANS, it will have become apparent in fore-going chapters, are a complicated people. An inhab-itant of the northern half of this continent may be at one and the same time Canadian, British, and North Ameri-can. Or he can be French, British, Canadian, and North American. Few could describe themselves simply as Ca-nadians, in the same sense that Americans can describe themselves as Americans, and talk of "the American way." Many have doubted whether there is such a thing as a Canadian.

Larger and older than the United States, richly if not so variously dowered, Canada finds herself after three hundred years with still undeveloped resources and less than a tenth of the population of her great neighbor. Her English and French Canadians have achieved, despite their long association, only what André Siegfried has called "a modus vivendi without cordiality." Three hundred thou-sand Americans and some 2,000,000 others of various Eu-ropean origin have leavened this mass without fusing it.

There is such a thing as a French-Canadian culture but no such thing as a Canadian culture. Canada has yet to achieve a literature. An American, Francis Parkman, was one of her best-known historians. A Frenchman, from

France, Louis Hémon, wrote the only great book that Canada has inspired. Probably the most distinguished figure in Canada's literary history is still Thomas Haliburton, who died seventy-five years ago. Significantly his most famous creation, comic Sam Slick, was a Yankee. The romantic history of Quebec was explored with monetary profit by Sir Gilbert Parker and some of his imitators, but, though the writers may have been enriched, literature was not. Canada is a noble and an austere land, in many ways like none other in the world. She is a nation in the making. But her writers have shown no true awareness of their country or her life and problems. None of her musicians has captured her rhythms as Sibelius did those of his little nation in *Finlandia*. With the single exception of painting, her art has been derivative. Her painters have been able to see their country though her writers and musicians could not. They have painted it, in its own hard and brilliant light and audacious color (an Englishman's reaction to the Canadian woods in autumn is that they are impossible and in any case not in good taste) and conveyed a true sense of its boundless distances, its harsh and massive architecture, its sharply accented rhythms. The writer remembers the impression produced on London when the famous "School of Seven," whose realistic rendition of the Canadian scene had been rejected in their own country as a libel on Canada, exhibited at the Wembley Exhibition there in 1924. One English critic acclaimed their work as "the most vital group of paintings produced since the war."

Canadians can see but they cannot analyze or synthesize. There is no Canadian drama and no such thing as a Canadian architecture. The mildest thing to be said about

Canadian taste in the nineties is that it was late Victorian. Since then there has been an improvement both in design and in furnishing, but it is the result of imitativeness, not origination.

Canada has actors, but they act for New York or Hollywood; singers, but they have sung—and one of them is supervising—at the Metropolitan. Her one unique accomplishment in the arts of entertainment, the Dionne quintuplets, was kept at home only by legislative act. Canada is more Roman than Greek. She has produced no philosophers and few artists but many warriors and statesmen. In Andrew Bonar Law, she gave a Prime Minister to England. But though she has bred many men of parts, the parts unfortunately have proved interchangeable, and Britain and the United States have benefited thereby.

Canada is a confederation but not a nation. Measured by the United States, she is a failure. She could never have been expected to equal the United States in population or industrial development, since she does not enjoy the latter's variety of natural resources, but she has resources enough for a population far larger than her present 11,-000,000. The 250,000,000 souls with whom Lloyd George, in a burst of after-dinner oratory, once peopled Canada's vast spaces will never find a habitation outside his Celtic imagination. But Canada, if she had kept step with the United States, would have a population of 40,000,000 today. Instead she finds herself sparsely populated and her people dangerously divided. Canada cannot call her soul her own. She has sacrificed much to remain British but she is failing even in this aspiration. She is slightly less than half British now, and in thirty years, unless something is done, her population will be more than 60 per cent non-British. By that time, by natural increase only, it will have grown to 16,600,000, according to the well-known authorities W. B. Hurd and M. C. McLean. In one hundred years, at its present rate of growth, it would total only 20,700,000.

Asked why his country's development is almost negligible compared with that of the United States, the average Canadian might blame its climate. But Russia, with a climate as severe as Canada's, has 180,000,000. On the other hand, the climate of the American Southern States has allowed a goodly proportion of their inhabitants to be debilitated by hookworm. Some Canadians contend that their country will not support more people. A university professor once told the writer that he did not believe Canada would have been able to maintain even her present standard of living had she not had the United States at hand to drain off her surplus population. But mineral discoveries in the past twenty years have indicated new sources of wealth in regions hitherto considered barren land, and Canada, unlike the United States, still has a frontier. Who would have dreamed twenty years ago that she would have become by now the world's principal source of platinum and radium, fourth largest supplier of gold? It is not in the poverty of her natural resources but in the lack of development of them beyond the most primary stages that Canada has suffered. Compared with the population of little England, her 11,000,000 people simply do not make sense.

In the opinion of this writer, the real reason for Canada's tardy growth is to be found partly in her spiritual dependence on Great Britain, which has often paralyzed her energies, but to a far greater extent in her geographical proximity to the United States. The United States has been a huge magnet which has drawn Canada's population tightly up against the border like so many iron filings. Canadians with even more iron in their blood have been drawn right across the border. The United States has been a happy hunting ground for Canadians but one from which, like that other happy hunting ground, they seldom returned. She has been a benevolent vampire draining Canada of her best product—her people—while refusing to buy her other goods unless they were indispensable raw materials. Her tariffs preserved Canada as a political and economic entity, while her free list for Canadians robbed that entity of substance. That, more than climate, explains why Canada's broad acres are still so thinly held. Her climate is certainly far more livable than Brazil's, yet Brazil has more than three times as many people.

Canada, like the United States, threw her doors open to Europe. Sir Wilfrid Laurier proclaimed enthusiastically that "the twentieth century belongs to Canada!" as Scandinavians and Germans and Slavs and Italians poured into the prairies from 1900 to 1914. In 1901 Canada's population was 5,370,000. By 1911 there had been a natural increase of 850,000 and immigration of 1,850,000. Canada should thus have had 8,000,000 people in 1911. Actually she had almost a million less. In the next decade the natural increase was 1,150,000 and immigration 1,729,000. She should have had 10,085,000 inhabitants in 1921 but she had only 8,790,000, and in 1931 she had only 10,370,000 when she should have had 11,600,000.

In thirty years Canada lost through emigration to the United States 70 per cent of her accretion through immigration from all sources, or 102 per cent of what she gained through natural increase. The net effect of migration on her was the exchange of native-born Canadians for European newcomers. Her policies have not only failed to keep Canada British but they have not kept Canadians at home. In 1871, 83 per cent of her population was native-born, in 1931 only 77 per cent. More than 16 per cent of all Canadian-born people and perhaps a third of the total Canadian stock are now living south of the border. Ten per cent of Canadian university graduates make their living in the United States—a serious loss of quality. To compare this with the 0.3 per cent of Canadians who were born in the United States is to appreciate the terrific pull of the American magnet.

It is doubtful whether the net effect of immigration has been to increase Canada's population at all since Confederation. French Canada has not benefited in the least from immigration, yet the proportion of French Canadians has steadily increased. The proportion of Canadians of British origin has dropped since 1901, although from 1918 to 1931 the immigration of approved settlers from Britain was assisted by the Canadian and British Governments.

Since the depression of 1930, immigration has been restricted to negligible proportions. Even when Europe's refugees, fleeing from before the new Attila, crowded every seaport and consular office in Europe seeking sanctuary across the Atlantic, Canada shut her heart and her doors to all but a very few. This held true of Aryan as well as Jew, of skilled as well as unskilled worker, of intellectual and craftsman. Probably never before has an unpeopled and undeveloped country been offered opportunity to acquire so many workers with special skills, so many teachers and scientists of high talent, the human nucleus of so many of the new industries she needs for diversification. A bold policy of acceptance and assimilation might have paid rich dividends in the not too far distant future. But short-range objections were allowed to outweigh long-term wisdom. In the whole matter of immigration, in fact, Canada finds herself on the horns of a dilemma. Because she has so few people in so large a territory, her manufacturing costs are high and her home market meager, making her dangerously dependent on a lessened international demand. But since the international market is depressed and her home market is meager, she will not accept new citizens because of the difficulty of placing them. Most of those she has accepted have been farmers for the prairies, although farming on the prairies has not been profitable for more than a decade.

Canada once proclaimed, and practiced, a National Policy. It was the invention of Sir John A. Macdonald, the Conservative leader who played the major part in bringing about Canadian Confederation, but he invented it only after he failed to obtain a reciprocity treaty with the United States. The National Policy was designed to create a home market for Canada's products by developing her own secondary industries behind a tariff wall. Its patriotic purpose was to preserve Canada's national identity. In practice it achieved both its aims in part, though the cost to Canada, it has been argued, was greater than the advantage.

The National Policy, in any case, has played—and over-played—its part. What Canada appears to need today is a new kind of National Policy, designed not only to people her empty acres, but to infuse the souls of those who people them with a strong sense of their identity with the land and with one another. More than her attachment to England, Canada's impelling motive for more than a hundred years was her fear and dislike of the United States. It formed the foundation of her national feeling. But now it has almost disappeared and Canada has found nothing to put in its place. Not yet quite vanished is the colonial mentality of English Canadians—the greatest obstacle to Canada's attainment of autonomous mental and emotional stature. It is the colonial mentality which has made Canada, alike for Great Britain and the United States, hard to live with. It has had many curious effects, all bad. It leads imperialist-minded Canadian editors to censor American-obtained news dispatches about British affairs and to treat any Canadian criticism of a particular act of a particular British Government as questioning the whole of Holy Writ. It has, perhaps, been responsible, in another direction, for that passive resistance to active co-operation with Great Britain of which the present Canadian Prime Minister is the most distinguished exponent. Canadian statesmen can be "natural" with their opposite numbers in Washington; few of them have ever been so in London.

If English-speaking Canadians could outgrow their colonialism they might be able to effect a real rapprochement with their French-Canadian fellow-citizens. It is obvious that such a rapprochement must be achieved before Canada can ever become a nation. As an example of harmonious co-operation of two races within a common political unit she is about on a par with Belgium, where the Walloons and the Flemings quarrel but do not part. But if she is to fulfill her destiny she must equal the achievement of Switzerland, where three races with mutually antagonistic traditions have co-operated to form one of the most single-minded of nations.

Uppermost in the mind of the French Canadian is the desire to stay French and Catholic. That being assured, he wishes to remain a Canadian. As an obstacle to his remaining French he fears the English Canadian less than he fears "Americanization." He does not need to fear the English Canadian, for he has lived with him for one hundred and seventy-seven years and, far from succumbing to him, he threatens to overwhelm him biologically. But if Canada ever joined the United States he knows that he would be swamped in an English-speaking sea. As it is, the flood of entertainment and propaganda that assails his ears in the form of American radio programs and his eyes in the shape of American films, magazines, and tabloids, the contagion of American materialism and this-worldliness that drifts across the frontier and has long since infected his English-Canadian compatriot, is a constant danger to his racial identity. Therefore, while English Canadians in moments of petulance with Great Britain have sometimes declared for annexation to the United States, the French Canadian has never done so.

Not because he desires to remain French and Catholic—for they are not concerned—but because he wishes to remain solely and simply Canadian he abhors Canada's participation in European wars although prepared to defend

Canadian soil as he has defended it in the past. It is for this reason that he can neither understand nor sympathize with the English Canadian who has been not only ready to lay down his own life for the furtherance of imperial ends which he has not helped to shape but to conscript his French-Canadian fellow-citizen to do so.

It will be seen that the French Canadian is in a dilemma. Canadian isolation would absolve him from the necessity of fighting wars abroad but greatly increase the danger of "Americanization." The minority rights which have assured him the free practice of his religion, his law, and his language were obtained from Britain, not from Canada, and might not be so secure, he sometimes fears, in an independent Canada. On the whole he would like to keep the British connection if only it did not mean participation in a war every quarter of a century.

As between Canada's recent procedure of drifting somnambulistically into a war which might have been averted by a more determined and intelligent strategy and a policy of active intervention in British affairs to shape them in the interests of the whole Commonwealth rather than in those of a Britain preoccupied with Europe, India, and her crown colonies, the intelligent French Canadian would probably choose the latter. A tactic which would give Canada the reality instead of the shadow of control over her external affairs might appeal to him, at least, as the better choice of two evils. It would enable him to play an active part in determining his own destiny rather than to maintain an attitude of passive resistance which has earned him the dislike of his English-speaking compatriots without achieving any other end. If he cannot detach them

from Britain he could help them detach Britain from
Europe. While Canada is part of a world empire compris-
ing more than a dozen distinct races and at least three-
score different languages and dialects, the French Canadian
need not feel out of place. In a strictly North American
Canada he becomes the great exception.

Canada has had many strokes of good luck in her economic progress. The World War, paradoxically, was one
of them. Those who bewail its legacies forget that it rescued Canada from the imminent onset of hard times. The
year 1913 had found her with nearly $200,000,000 to pay
in annual interest and dividend charges, a $300,000,000
adverse trade balance, and a sudden damming-up, because
of financial stringency and overborrowing, of the stream
of foreign lending from London on which she had de-
pended for five years. She was faced with the violent read-
justment if not the complete dislocation of her economy.
And then came the war, which, whatever else it did, gave
her another sixteen years of growth before the onset of the
Great Slump of 1930.

The present war may have saved her from an even worse
situation. It found the timbers of Confederation cracking
ominously while the chilly breath of disunion blew
through the widening chinks and the sound of wrangling
voices reached an ever more scandalous pitch. It found
the creditor industrial East arrayed against the debtor
agricultural West. For long eastern industry had looked
west for its indispensable market. Now the West, which
was in essence a gamble in export wheat, had lost that
gamble. The East, having found a better gamble in mining for export, was grumbling against being used—as

Premier Hepburn of Ontario put it—as a "milch cow" for
the drought-stricken, market-bereft prairies. Stung, the
prairies had retaliated with such moves as Alberta's Social
Credit experiment and the formation in Saskatchewan of
a party to promote a separate British state in Western
Canada. Aided by a series of British Privy Council decisions which had stripped the Federal Government of its
residuary power to settle matters of national interest, the
provinces had been asserting an ever-increasing independence, and Liberal Premier Hepburn had united in bizarre
fellowship with Conservative Premier Duplessis of Quebec
to decry and defeat the policies of Prime Minister Mackenzie King. French Canada had set up a paternalistic regime
with Fascist trimmings in defiance of the spirit, at least,
of Canadian law. French Canadian nationalism, in new
and militant trappings, seemed again on the march. Sir
Evelyn Wrench, student of imperial affairs and promoter
of imperial fellowship, had come over from London to
take a look at it all and gone back to be quoted as saying
that Confederation was an absurdity; neither economically
nor geographically was Canada an entity; the real Canada
was the St. Lawrence area which should be a French-
speaking dominion and the rest of Canada should either
become local dominions or be absorbed by the United
States.

A stranger finding himself in this prewar Canada might
have concluded that her collapse was imminent. Actually
what sounded like the premonitors of an earthquake were
the rumblings of an empty stomach. It was the old story
of poverty coming in at the door and love flying out of
the window. After seven lean years the Canadian was in a

mood to grumble and to lay the blame for his hard fate on his next-door neighbor. For the politician not too scrupulous to exploit it, the occasion obviously promised well and it found in seats of provincial power two past masters in the art of such exploitation. The situation, if prolonged, might have grown to be dangerous. But the war came and stilled all this domestic riot and commotion.

If the war results directly or indirectly in a transatlantic exodus of British industry and population it may prove to be another ill wind that blows Canada good. Another 5,000,000 readily assimilable citizens would solve most of the problems that trouble her today. It would, of course, bring new problems. There might be a struggle with the newcomers for the possession of Canada. It would be ended in short order. It was the progenitors of some of the stanchest and most distinguished imperialists to be found today among the English-speaking population of Montreal who in 1849 issued a manifesto in favor of American annexation and burned down the Parliament Buildings as a mark of their displeasure with the English Government—an action which resulted in the transfer of the seat of authority to Ottawa. They assaulted Lord Elgin, the English governor-general, in the streets and demanded his recall. All this indignation was caused by his signature of a bill indemnifying the loyal French population of Lower Canada for the losses suffered in the Rebellion of 1837. The British Loyalists had also been indemnified but they wanted a monopoly of redress. Eleven years earlier, when Lord Elgin's father-in-law, the gifted Lord Durham, had recommended responsible government for Canada the Loyalists of Upper Canada exploded into wrath, and orated in-

dignantly about "the reward" of treason. Lord Durham's
report was described in a diary of that time as having
"unquestionably reanimated the drooping courage of the
traitorous and of the exiles in the United States, and
kindled anew the almost extinct sympathies of their
American friends, who have engraved the name of Lord
Durham on the blades of their bowie knives in demonstration of their idea of the certain result of 'Responsible
Government.' " The real trouble about responsible government was that it threatened to make office and patronage accessible to the majority where they had been a
monopoly for the upper-class Loyalists.

The Canadian loyalist has been accustomed to see that
his loyalty paid dividends. It would be amusing to witness
the mental metamorphosis of the Toronto imperialist—
there is a saying in Canada that when Toronto is in danger the Empire is in danger—faced by the prospect of having some of the more lately arrived boys of the bulldog
breed muscle in on his patriotic preserves. The experience
might be good for both parties concerned.

It is always easier to let things happen than to make
things happen. People will accept as the logic of events
what they will not see planned for. But if the war does
not settle Canada's troubles in some such way as indicated
it would seem that she must take her own future in hand.
Her development has hitherto been left largely to free
enterprise and the play of international forces in so far as
they could operate over her tariff walls. They have not
sufficed. If Canada is to have more people it looks as if she
must plan for them. She has made some very respectable
experiments in co-operation such as the western wheat

pools, the People's Banks in Quebec province, and the Nova Scotia Credit Unions. To judge from the Ontario Hydro-Electric Commission and the government-owned Temiskaming and Northern Ontario Railway she plans well when she goes in for it. She is planning now because she is at war. She has assembled at Ottawa some of the brightest business minds in the country and they have co-ordinated her war efforts with a minimum of friction. To reassure the leaders of private enterprise the Government borrowed the co-ordinators from them rather than from the civil service or the universities. The movement of capital and of essential exports has been placed under strict supervision, the provision and price of food supplies have been made subject to control, industry has been mobilized to supply her own and her Allies' needs, and money is to be found through taxation and government loans at low interest rates to pay for all this.

A country which can do this for a European war which she never wanted or provoked might decide some day to do it for her own peaceful development at home. It would not be in entire accordance with the *laissez faire* philosophy of her present Prime Minister, but then neither is fighting a war in strict alignment with his precept on that subject. One could imagine Mr. King, that malleable man, prolonging planning if he thought a majority could be found for it. To expect leadership from him in this direction might be asking too much, but it is not beyond the range of probability that he might quite cheerfully consent to be dragged backward into a planned future.

In any event, if only Canada can make up her mind what she wants her future to be, there need be little doubt of her ability to achieve it. A people which could live next door for so long to so powerful and proselytizing a nation as the United States and yet keep its national faith; which could be washed over by so constant a stream of Americanizing influences pouring across the border in the form of newspapers, magazines, tourists, films, and the radio, and yet keep its head above water, must have vitality and willpower. If the United States has drained Canada of some of her best blood, the process may soon be reversed. The people of this continent have long been accustomed, when opportunity beckons, to follow it across the boundary lines—and Canada still has a frontier. The United States, to all appearances, has almost reached the saturation point: Canada is far from it. When Canada's hour strikes she will benefit from the proximity of the United States where she has suffered from it. She will be glad to have at her open door such an immense reservoir of capital, manpower, and technical resources. Americans have proved just as assimilable in Canada as Canadians in the United States. As immigrants they might be described as predigested. It was a flood of newcomers from the revolutionary United States that gave Canada its first great impetus to growth. From a staid and settled United States may come its next.

PART III

The Economic
Aspect

12

Canada Is a Mighty Land

CANADA represents politics at war with geography. She is geographically an integral part of the American continent. She is sharply divided into four distinct sections and the divisions are vertical ones. But politically she belongs to a system mainly European and her economy has been organized not on a north-south but on an east-west axis. Therein lies in part the explanation of Canada's slow progress, of her lack of unity, of her present discontents.

Canada is the third largest country in the world. Only Russia and China are larger, although the United States with its dependencies covers a little more territory. Canada has an area almost as great as Europe's. She is more than a quarter of the whole British Empire and she could drown Great Britain in her Great Lakes. She is bounded on the east by the Atlantic, on the west by the Pacific, on the south by the United States, and on the north by the North Pole. She has no trouble in obeying that ancient recipe of health: Keep your head cool and your feet warm.

But she has trouble in growing up. In all the world there are few territories so thinly held as Canada's. She has too much geography and it is not even all of one piece. Canada consists of the Maritime Provinces, of the St. Lawrence Valley, of the western prairies, and of British Columbia. Between the Maritime Provinces and the St. Lawrence Valley, for twenty-four hours of train travel, is a region unproductive and sparsely populated. Between Toronto and Winnipeg is a thousand miles of rock, river, lake, and forest. The Rocky Mountains rear their heads far into the sky to divide the prairies from the coastal province of British Columbia.

All these regions find natural prolongations south of the largely artificial border that divides Canada from the United States and are far more closely related to them than to each other. The resemblance is not only geographic. In the Maritime Provinces and the eastern townships of Quebec a New Englander finds himself almost at home. Not only are famous New England names perpetuated there but he finds age, conservatism, a conviction that their fishing, farming, lumbering, and trading interests had been sacrificed fiscally for the benefit of the industrialized Central Canada and a tendency to supply more than a proportionate share of the Dominion's public and professional notables. There is little about Ontario that seems strange to the upstate New Yorker. He finds it wealthy, highly industrialized, progressive, and self-satisfied. A farmer from the Dakotas could blunder across the border into Saskatchewan without noticing the difference. He would find the same broad prairies, the same alternation of growth and drought, the same distrust of the banking and manufacturing East, the same readiness for legislative and monetary experiment. In other words, he would find the Canadian West not only a geo-

graphical expression but a state of mind. Still farther west
a northward-faring American would discover that the
Pacific climate does not lose its charm across the Canadian
boundary, nor does the Douglas fir cast less shade than the
Oregon pine.

But though the American might feel at home in Canada's Maritimes, her St. Lawrence Valley, or her prairies,
he would be puzzled by the semi-wilderness that separates
them, for that is a strictly Canadian phenomenon known
as the Laurentian, or Canadian Shield. On a map of the
Dominion the Laurentian Shield looks like a stony hand
clutching the throat of Hudson Bay, with a thumb cover-
ing the whole of Labrador and clenched fingers reaching
north to the Arctic Ocean. The Laurentian Shield is Canada's hard fate. It occupies more than two-thirds of her
whole area. Except for the lowlands south of Hudson Bay,
the southern sections of Ontario and Quebec and the
Maritime Provinces, the whole eastern half of Canada is
covered or underlain by the Pre-Cambrian rocks, the oldest on the earth's surface. The Pre-Cambrian formations
are the product of earth's remotest agonies. They are so
ancient that they antedated life and they are hostile to life
today. A subdued and deeply eroded plateau, with two or
three lakes gemming its every square mile and a succession of low, rocky hills standing blue against every horizon,
the Laurentian Shield is a shield with a bar sinister. In its
northern areas nothing can be grown. Its southern area is
covered by coniferous forests but has only pockets of till-
able land. Both timber and land are generally hard to get
at, since the rivers that run through the deep crevices in

the Shield, though splendid potential sources of hydro-electric power, are too rapid-strewn and swift for navigation except by canoe.

That was the Laurentian Shield as Canadians knew it a quarter-century ago. But in the words of the late Lord Tweedsmuir, who said so many things so well, "the Laurentian Shield, once regarded as a desert useless to man, is now seen to be the lid of an amazing treasure house." Twenty-five years ago it was Canada's great interior plain, which stretches west from the Laurentian Shield, east from the Rockies, and north from the American border to the Arctic, which seemed to be her promised land. There the golden flood of wheat was rolling—as Canada's cerealists evolved ever more quickly maturing varieties—decade by decade further northward. But wheat is at a discount in this autarchic world. It is the gold and silver and nickel and copper and zinc and platinum of the Laurentian plateau that have become Canada's export mainstay and are pushing her frontiers northward. It was they that rescued her economy from the Great Depression. Though a world preparing for war did not want wheat it wanted minerals. Though little could grow in the thin layer of soil that covers the deeply glaciated Pre-Cambrian rocks, the world's fourth largest gold deposits lay there for the mining. When Canada threw a link of steel from east to west to bind her provinces into one confederation it had cost half a million dollars a mile to blast the Canadian Pacific Railway through that rock north of Lake Superior. Critics of the project had said it was "a piece of madness" to lay track through such a wilderness. But the madness of 1885 has become the sanity of today. The 5,000,000 tons of nickel and copper ore in the Mond Levack mine would alone pay for the road which taps them.

When masses of molten rock intruded between older strata in the course of those successive convulsions that have formed the earth's surface they gave off, while cooling, mineralizing solutions which hardened into ore deposits. That is what happened in the Pre-Cambrian Shield. It was extensively and repeatedly invaded by masses of igneous granite and diabase and other intrusions. It was this fiery mating that created the nickel-copper deposits of Sudbury, the silver-cobalt ores of Cobalt and its sister camps, the zinc-copper ores of Northern Manitoba, the pitchblende and silver deposits of Great Bear Lake, and the deposits of mica, graphite, feldspar, magnesite, fluorite, kaolin, molybdenite, talc, and apatite of Eastern Ontario and Western Quebec.

Canada has three of the greatest rivers on the North American continent. Unfortunately, of the three one, the Mackenzie, flows north for 2500 miles to the Arctic Ocean and another, the Saskatchewan, rises in the Rockies and ends in the almost equally arctic Hudson Bay. The country is so tilted that most of its rivers flow away from the settled areas toward the regions of ice and snow. They would be much more useful if they ran in the opposite direction but nature seems to have indicated plainly to Canadians that theirs must be a northern fate.

If it is their fate they have not yet accepted it in any mass manner. Inhabited Canada is a thin and interrupted band paralleling the American border. North of any section of it the visiting American could find what he has lost in his own country—the frontier. The frontier, the Never

Never country, the land of the second chance, the place
where all will be put right. It is fringed in the Northwest
with wheat and in the Northeast with gold. Beyond there
is still more land, a sub-Arctic wilderness where even the
ground birch gives way to tundra and the Indian yields
place to the Eskimo. It is inhabited, besides its two races
of aborigines, by missionaries, fur-traders, wireless opera-
tors, Mounted Policemen, and, of late years, prospectors.
Oil has been found on the Mackenzie River near Fort
Norman. The pitchblende deposits of Great Bear Lake
were discovered only ten years ago but already they have
cut the world price of radium by more than half. The
Yellowknife River in the Great Slave Lake area has produced one of the most promising gold strikes of recent
times. Nickel has been discovered on the eastern arm of
Great Slave Lake and the west coast of Hudson Bay. If
there is the making of a mining industry in Canada's sub-
Arctic there is the possibility of a secondary agricultural
industry to support it. From a Dominion Experimental
Substation at Beaverlodge, Alberta, have come reports of
significant cropping results along the Mackenzie water system "north of sixty." Crab apples have ripened on ten-
foot trees on the shore of Great Slave Lake, 526 miles
north of Edmonton. Potato vines at Fort Simpson (latitude 61° 52′ north) grew an inch and a half a day in early
July, doubling their height in a week. Beyond the Arctic
Circle potatoes have yielded 300 and 400 bushels an acre.
In two years cereals have ripened in the Mackenzie delta
well enough to reproduce.

Those who would visit Canada's sub-Arctic in winter

must travel either by one of the oldest means of transportation or by the newest—the dogsled or the airplane.
In summer they may lounge their way by steamboat a distance of more than 1600 miles from the end of steel at
Waterways, Alberta, to the Arctic Ocean with but one interruption—the rapids between Fitzgerald and Fort Smith.
The round-trip takes thirty-three days. By airplane almost
any part of the mainland of Northern Canada, and many
of its Arctic islands, can be reached in two or three days
from the end of steel. Why go so far to see Canada's "barren lands"? But those who know them say they are not
barren lands but Arctic prairies, where there is always
plant life of some kind, where heather blooms on the hill-
tops and in the upland valleys luxuriant meadows supply
the caribou with summer feed. Lord Tweedsmuir wrote
enthusiastically of the "antiseptic air" that blows above
them. In 1931 less than a thousand white men breathed it.
No one knows how many there are now, but their number
has been increasing fast. There seems no reason to doubt
that Canada's Western Arctic would prove at least as hos-
pitable to man as Russia's Siberia.

Meanwhile Canada takes her Arctic very seriously. She
claims everything north of her territories and annually
sends an Eastern Arctic Patrol ship on a tour of inspection
and exploration. Sometimes she sends one up from her
western coast and they meet to perpetuate the tradition of
the Northwest Passage. The Arctic interests her not only
because it is the source of much of her weather and a
potential source of coal and other minerals but because it
will some day be the great aerial short cut between Asia

and Europe and America. Obviously Canada is destined
to be the air crossroads of the world. The shortest way
from Europe to China lies across her territories. By that
path—London to Newfoundland, to Edmonton, to Alaska,
across the Bering Strait and down the eastern coast of
Siberia—Shanghai is 4000 miles nearer than by the route
now being flown from New York across the Pacific. It
would avoid the long water hop across the Pacific and
would allow profitable pay loads to be borne in machines
of moderate cost. Already it is being flown as far as White-
horse in the Yukon, and its extension awaits only the coming of peace. Meanwhile Canadians have learned all they
need to know about northern flying. Though it lacks bea-
cons, lighted airways, and even landing fields there is an
Arctic airmail. The flying in of prospectors, miners, and
even mining machinery is an old story in the North and
now the Hudson's Bay Company and Revillon Frères have
begun to use airplanes to gather in their fur catches. Canada already carries more freight by air than any other
country in the world.

Two transcontinental railroads serve the Canadian
prairies, one of the world's great granaries. There "Number One Hard," the finest wheat in the world, is grown.
But growing it is a gamble and it is one against which
nature and man of late years have stacked the cards. For
some six years past a succession of droughts and dust
storms has devastated the prairie provinces and particularly
Saskatchewan. Give Saskatchewan a few inches of rainfall
and a rising market and there is no part of the world that
will render richer and quicker returns to the farmer. But,
as will be explained in the succeeding chapter, with Sas-

katchewan it is wheat "or else . . ." Large areas have had
to be abandoned in the past few years. Others may be
saved by irrigation but the possibilities of irrigation in the
prairies are limited. It has become obvious that the West
was too hastily settled, that its good land, far from being
limitless, has already been largely taken up. It has been
demonstrated that the short growing season and limited
rainfall make mixed farming impossible, that wheat is the
only satisfactory crop, and that it demands large-scale
farming methods—a highly mechanized agriculture using
machinery rather than men and not an intensive hus-
bandry giving a high return for human labor. Gone are
the days when thousands of men flocked from Eastern
Canada, from the United States, and even from Great
Britain to help the western farmer harvest his crop. Only
in Prince Edward Island, in the valleys of Nova Scotia and
New Brunswick, in the St. Lawrence Valley, the older
parts of Ontario, and the valleys of British Columbia is a
more intensive type of agriculture possible in Canada.
Probably 90 per cent of Canada's total land area is un-
suited for profitable farming. Of the remaining 10 per
cent about a third is now under crop.

There is another valuable crop which Canada produces.
That is its forests, which stretch from the Atlantic to the
Pacific and northward from the American boundary to
beyond the Arctic Circle. Canada's forest area has been
estimated at 1,225,000 square miles, or a third of its land
area. Of this, about 1,000,000 square miles can best be
utilized under forest and of that vast area only about
360,000 square miles is accessible and produces timber of
merchantable size today. Another 400,000 square miles

will produce it eventually. Eastern Canada has 67 per cent of this area, British Columbia 18 per cent, and the three prairie provinces between them only 14 per cent. Of the merchantable trees, 95 per cent are coniferous, only Russia and the United States having coniferous forests that equal Canada's. Depletion has been estimated at 3.3 per cent a year, and since 90 per cent of Canada's forest area is still owned by the Federal Government or the provincial governments there is no reason why conservation measures should not ensure a permanent crop. But as things are at present there is going on what Canadian authorities call a "considerable net depletion." As forest products form a quarter of Canada's total exports, being exceeded only by the products of the farm, this is important.

Since Canada is vertically cleft geographically, climatically, and economically and since her agriculture and industry are within a 200-mile haul of the American market practically at any point, the fact that she trades east and west instead of north and south seems to be a victory achieved by politics at the expense of economics. But there is one tremendous qualification of this generalization—the St. Lawrence–Great Lakes water system. Jacques Cartier, who discovered the St. Lawrence, called it the "River of Canada." He was speaking more prophetically than he knew, for the St. Lawrence is Canada. Canada is the result of the St. Lawrence as Egypt is the result of the Nile. The seeds of Canadian nationality were sown on its banks and watered by its flood. There they sprouted and flourished and there they remained until word came that the prairies —the Great Lone Land of the trapper and the trader— would grow wheat at the first touch of the plow. Then the course of Canadian colonization leaped a thousand miles westward. But still the St. Lawrence served it, for over the river and its chain of great lakes poured a new current of wheat on its way to the markets of Europe.

Since the earliest advent of the white man the St. Lawrence has been the gateway to Canada and the pathway of empire. Up its mighty stream passed in turn the Indians, the French explorers, missionaries, and traders, and the British conquerors. Now the ships of all the world breast its current on their way to Montreal, the world's largest inland seaport. If the St. Lawrence Seaway project is realized—it would be better to say "when," for its execution is only a matter of time and its delay the last stand of vested interest—they will dock at Fort William and Port Arthur, in the very heart of Canada.

Then the St. Lawrence, which for almost its whole length is in Canadian territory, will assume an even greater importance in Canada's economy. It will link her still more inevitably with the sea and with the lands that lie across it. It will strengthen her east-west axis. Canada became French because of the St. Lawrence and the habitant still clings close to its shores today. But without the St. Lawrence Canada could not have remained British. The southward pull was tremendous but her great window on the world looked eastward. Nature, which had otherwise designed Canada as a northward prolongation of this continent, had pointed one finger at Europe and Canada has followed it to her fate. It is not for nothing, obviously, that the St. Lawrence flows eastward and the Mississippi south.

The St. Lawrence drains a territory of 500,000 square miles which contains half the fresh water in the world.

The Mississippi and the Hudson together pour no such tribute into the sea. It is mighty in its source, Lake Superior, the largest fresh water lake on the surface of the globe and in its consummation, where it kisses the sea with a mouth ninety miles wide. On its 2000-mile course from the fresh water to the salt, it takes one gigantic leap, Niagara, which moves the dynamos and the soul of man, pauses to play among the emerald-tipped granite and gneiss fretwork which is the Thousand Islands, and bathes the feet of the Laurentians before the moment when, taking Anticosti like a bit in its teeth, it gallops white-maned into the Gulf that also bears its name. The same irresistible compulsion that moves the St. Lawrence has moved the Canadians who dwelt along its banks. Of their railroads the two greatest run east and west. Another runs to Hudson Bay, the third eastern gateway of this continent. The New England and Chicago extensions of the Canadian National Railways, the passage of the Canadian Pacific Railway through American territory in New England and the Northwest and of the New York Central, Wabash, and Pere Marquette Railways across Ontario, give Canada and the United States a network of international links possessed by no other two countries in the world. But it is overpowered by the east-west trackage of the C.P.R. and of the Canadian National, which is two transcontinental roads in one, by the St. Lawrence–Great Lakes water system, and by the Panama Canal, which is an eastern waterway for Canada's Pacific coast.

Canada is a vast and lonely land. It will always be so, for even if her population triples in the next century how can 35,000,000 people possess a territory as large as hers except in name? She is gigantically framed and wildly clad. In Europe nature has come to be the natural and im-memorial setting of mankind. In the United States she is man's reflection and resentful victim. In Canada she is scarcely yet aware of him and even when aware she looks over his head. There are awing distances in Canada, vast freedoms, immense silences. There are rushing rivers and lonely, loon-haunted lakes where no angler ever yet cast a lure, silent forests where the moose abounds in Gothic majesty and the lumbering bear has not learned to fear the crack of a rifle. A vast forest zone stretching across the continent provides an immense habitat for game and birds. Caribou, the Rocky Mountain sheep, and the Rocky Mountain goat, almost extinct in the United States, flourish still in Canada. Years ago the Dominion and provincial gov-ernments withdrew from settlement thousands of square miles of the finest game territory in Canada and converted them into national parks and forests. These tremendous territories are closed to the hunter but open to the camper and fisher and holiday-maker generally. There are Jasper and Banff Parks in the Rockies; Elk Island Park in Alberta, where the elk and the buffalo roam in their fenced-in sanctuary; the Thousand Islands, Georgian Bay, Point Pelée, and Algonquin National Parks in Ontario; Fort Anne Park in Nova Scotia, where a thriving settlement existed before the Pilgrim Fathers landed at Plymouth Rock and whence in 1775 occurred the expulsion of the Acadians.

Because she has more space than she can ever fill and

more scenery than she knows what to do with, Canada has become increasingly a place of resort for the 130,000,000-odd inhabitants of the United States. A few years ago she became conscious of the fact that the tourist industry had become her fourth largest, that the 15,000,000 Americans who came annually across her borders were leaving some $250,000,000 to $300,000,000 of good American dollars behind them, that in her holiday facilities she had a potential source of wealth greater than that of her gold mines, greater even than that of her export wheat crop. It was not only the most important single item in Canada's balance of payments but a pleasing example of the workings of the great law of compensation, since her attractiveness to the tourist was a virtue of her defects. Where not many could live, many would play. Even her winter, she discovered eventually, was a tourist asset. There was a time when Canada was sensitive about her winter. It was this feeling which made Kipling's tribute to "Our Lady of the Snows" one of those things that might have been better expressed and led to the discouragement of Ice Palaces on the ground that they might be mistaken for the normal, not merely the gala, habitation of Canadians in January. In those days one of Canada's chief activities was immigration and there was a feeling that snow and cold would not allure immigrants.

But now Canada's immigrants are tourists, and some of them like it cold. Of winter Canadians have discovered that, far from being bad for business, there is money in it. Canadians themselves have come to look on their winter with friendlier eyes. Perhaps the greatest single factor in this has been the advent of skis, which have winged their heels and made them free of the fastnesses of frost and snow. Worshiped on his own altars, winter has been found a generous deity, to serve whom is to defy gravity, to breathe champagne, and to be warmed by flaming sunsets. Winter in Canada has become big business and with each year becomes a bigger business still.

Twilight of the Wheatfields

CANADA has been known as an important agricultural country for a hundred years and as the world's
leading exporter of wheat for the past twenty. Agriculture
is still her basic industry, although it is fast losing its place
to mining as a source of export. Nearly 40 per cent of
Canadian males who work at anything work on the farm.
In the prairie provinces most men are farmers. But they
don't make much money.

The story of agriculture in Eastern Canada is one of
slow but fairly steady growth. An increasing population
has absorbed an increasing production, so that exports of
cheese, butter, cattle, hides, and other products of mixed
farming, which once played a relatively important part in
Canada's balance of trade, scarcely increased at all in forty
years. Eastern farmers did not get rich, at least not quickly,
but neither did they starve.

The story of agriculture in Western Canada is a story
of wheat and there was nothing either slow or stable about
it. It began in the 1890's. The eastern farmer who had only
marginal land or none began to move west, and hard on
his heels came a rush of land-hungry peasants from Europe. They took up land wherever they could find it and
two transcontinental railroads followed them in the same

helter-skelter manner. When the World War began, Canada was already supplying 14 per cent of the world's import wheat requirements. Six years after the war was over she was supplying 48 per cent. Europe's quotas, tariffs, domestic subsidies, and exchange regulations, all designed to protect its own peasants from this flood of mass-produced hard wheat pouring across the Atlantic and to achieve a maximum of autarchy in preparation for the next war, cut Canada's share down to 30 per cent. In some years Argentina, because it is willing to sell cheaper, has surpassed her. The British market has been her great standby but even the British millers have been teaching their customers to eat a bread with less Canadian hard wheat and more of the cheaper, softer kinds.

Not only was their market cut down but the prairie wheat-growers found that they were being required to pay for mortgages, agricultural implements, and other necessities based on $2 wheat with wheat worth only a fraction of that. In 1921 the price was $2.21 a bushel. In two years it dropped to $1.08. But in 1930 it reached the catastrophic low of 53 cents. The purchasing power of prairie farmers was cut down to less than a third. Then came years of drought. In some of the best growing areas in Saskatchewan farmers saw five dry years succeed one another and the loosened topsoil finally disappear on the wings of a dust cloud. Now nothing will grow but the tough prairie grass, if that. The western farmer was peculiarly helpless in the face of such a sequence of calamities. Wheat and oats were his only crops. He had few cows or chickens and grew little or no fruit or vegetables. As often as not, canned goods supplied his table. If he did have a few cattle, he found that he did not have feed for them.

In his good days he had been an optimist and a specu-
lator, a land-miner rather than a farmer, a businessman in
agriculture. In the East they accused him of having spent
his money on trips to California and college educations
for his children instead of saving for the lean years. There
is nothing that shocks the eastern urbanite more than the
western farmer's sinful extravagance. Actually the number
of prairie vacationists in California was negligible but
there is no doubt that the western grain-grower had over-
bought the future in the twenties as lightheartedly as the
eastern businessman.

And now the businessman in agriculture threatens to
become a member of an agrarian proletariat. In 1921 more
than 85 per cent of all Canadian farms were owned by
their cultivators but after the 1930 depression there was a
decided growth of tenancy as mortgage after mortgage was
foreclosed. By means of a Farm Loan Act, a Farmers' Cred-
itors Arrangement Act, a Prairie Farm Rehabilitation Act,
and the setting up, just before the present war, of a government scheme for re-financing mortgages the Federal
Government did what it could to check this process. For
five years the R. B. Bennett government pegged wheat prices
although in the process it accumulated a 225,000,000-bushel
wheat surplus and finally stood threatened by a loss of
$50,000,000. Mr. Mackenzie King's government, when it
came to office, promptly sold out and, thanks to rising
prices in 1936, the loss was much smaller than had been
apprehended. Having sold out, the King government had
to adopt remedial measures of its own, such as a minimum
domestic price and a crop bonus. It has begun irrigation

projects and moved some farmers off submarginal lands. In Alberta Mr. Aberhart's government arbitrarily slashed mortgage interest rates and in Manitoba and Saskatchewan the mortgage companies themselves scaled them down. Despite these various forms of assistance, nearly one-third of the farming population in Saskatchewan was on government relief in 1939 and had been for some years. It sits on its dried-out farms and waits—waits for the one good year, with 30 inches of rain and no rust, or hail, or locusts, which will be the last throw to pay for all. Perhaps the war will bring it, although the war demand so far has been disappointing.

Canada's future, for a generation past, has been predicated on an expanding wheat market and its contraction was felt throughout her whole economic fabric. In the five post-depression years the gross agricultural income of the prairie provinces dropped from $4,327,000,000 to $1,997,000,000, a decline of 54 per cent. In the fifteen years from 1920 to 1935 the value of farm lands was cut exactly in two. The East, which had exploited the West, now discovered that it was supporting it. It was a bitter blow to the holder of western mortgages and to the railroads, which had invested 17,000 miles of track in the wheat country. It was bitterer still for the farmer and his friends. Thanks to that brilliant botanist, Dr. Charles Saunders, and his successors, Canada had originated first the famous Marquis wheat and then the Prelude, Ruby, Reward, and Garnet varieties, each of which ripened a little earlier and pushed the limit of settlement farther and farther north. When the depression came, wheat was being grown in the Peace River Valley, in Alberta, 600 miles north of the American boundary. The Peace River, with its great area of virgin soil, was perhaps the last agricultural frontier North America will know.

Because of what has happened to the wheat market, the western farmer has lost much of his economic and political importance in Canada. But his co-operative instinct has survived the depression. Perhaps because as a one-crop farmer he knows himself to be insecure he has shown an ability to organize uncommon among his individualistic kind. Ever since the formation of the Grain Growers' Grain Company in 1906 he has tended to unite against his natural allies-and-enemies, the railroads and the elevator companies. Alberta and Manitoba farmers formed the United Grain Growers and the Saskatchewan farmers formed the Saskatchewan Co-operative. These not only operated elevators but purchased flour, lumber, fence posts, wire, binder twine, coal, and farm machinery for their members. In 1923 wheat pools were formed in the three provinces and a central sales agency was organized to market the wheat of all three. In 1929 they owned a third of all the elevator space in the West, had become the world's largest producers' co-operative, and comprised half the prairie farmers. The depression hit the pools hard but they have survived and are apparently in the West to stay. To those who believe that the co-operative may be the happy medium between capitalism and socialism they are a heartening development.

The peasant is valued in Europe as a stabilizing element politically and economically. But farming in the Canadian West has represented anything but stability, either for the farmer or for the country. The eastern agriculturist, with his mixed crops and his home market, is far more secure economically and dependable politically. The French-Canadian habitant is perhaps the nearest thing to a peasant to be found in North America. And he is also, on occasion, still a pioneer, the farmer with an ax. His ambition is never to mine his land for a quick profit, still less to sell it, but to live on it and to leave it to his sons after him. His strip farm along the St. Lawrence, which still crowds its neighbors as in the days when the warwhoop of the Iroquois heralded the chief hazard of agriculture, is seldom more than 100 acres in extent. But he lives off it with the aid of his wife and children. Not for him the reapers and harvesters and combines of the West, nor the hope of sudden riches. But he always has a crop, he always has enough to feed himself, he has a home and a way of living.

The eastern farmer is coming to depend more and more on the home market. But he still produces enough cheese to make Canada the second or third largest exporter. The shipment of live cattle to England, once important, has declined and the United States now furnishes the principal market. Canada is a large exporter of bacon and ham to Great Britain but has never specialized in either as she has in wheat or as her Irish and Danish competitors have done. She once exported butter largely but now New Zealand butter competes on occasion in the Canadian home market, to the indignation of Canadian dairymen.

It is not the future of the eastern farmer that worries Canada's bankers and statesmen but what fate holds in store for the West. The present war is likely to improve the world market and the world wheat price for some years to come. An active instead of a static war will take men

away from the European wheat fields where it does not
devastate them. Shipment from the Danubian Basin may
be interrupted as it was in the World War. Wheat cargoes
will go down under German submarine warfare. Canada's
wheat can more readily be transported than that of her
competitors, since Halifax, one of her two winter ports on
the Atlantic, is the western base of the convoy system. Her
wheat will thus enjoy an advantage in Allied markets. After
the war the European peasant will return to his land as he
returned before. That is his immemorial way of life, a
moral law stronger than the laws of economics. But there
are some long-term factors in the world wheat situation
that promise favorably for Canada's grain-growers.

Russia, which supplied 24 per cent of the world's wheat
requirements before the World War, has passed out of the
export picture as a result of her increasing industrialization. Her exit greatly eases the situation. The United States,
from which Europe obtained 16 per cent of its wheat before the war and 22 per cent in 1925, tends to pass out of
the export field also as her population increases and the
law of diminishing returns applies. If the white man, or
perhaps it is the white woman, tends to eat less bread the
yellow man is eating more. If the European wheat demand
during the World War and for a few years after was abnor-
mal, so has been Europe's rejection of transatlantic wheat
since. It is hard to imagine ersatz autarchy surviving the
present war. According to international wheat experts there
has not been for some five years past a real overproduction
of cereals. A good deal of such production as there has
been has been forced, and therefore uneconomic, production.

If costs of production are kept low enough to compete with the Argentine, Canadian wheat will probably always be sure of a market in Europe. But the tendency will be toward larger farms, more mechanization. Perhaps collective farms, of the co-operative not the state type, will make their appearance in the West, together with the development of industry and a steady drift of farmers' sons into it. Submarginal land will revert to grass and settled areas will tend to draw together, making administration and education less expensive.

For the Canadian West already wears clothes far too big for her. They were designed to grow up in and instead she has shrunk. According to the 1931 census the area of farm land then occupied was 163,000,000 acres. But the total area under field crops or pasturage has been less than 65,-000,000 acres for the past fifteen years. If all the farms in the three prairie provinces had been grouped they could have been accommodated in any one of them. Fewer railroads would have been needed, fewer roads, fewer schools and churches, fewer governments. If wheat should come into its own again and the West triple its inhabitants, it will still have enough hotels and public buildings to serve them without erecting any more. The Manitoba Legislative Buildings would grace any capital in Europe, and Winnipeg, which has them, also has two huge hotels, either of which would have satisfied the yearnings of a cinquecento magnifico. Edmonton and Calgary, each with less than 100,000 citizens, also have caravansaries whose architects were obviously anxious to do something for posterity. They are dream castles erected on a basis of $2 wheat.

It is as a result of this discounting of the future that

Manitoba's public debt charges were 47 per cent of the provincial budget in 1936, the net public debt of Saskatchewan was 64 per cent of the annual income of all its inhabitants, and Winnipeg had to take over a third of all the property within its confines for tax delinquencies. Agriculture represented nearly two-thirds of net production in the prairie provinces and when it languished they languished.

But because it produces the hardest wheat Canada will remain one of the world's great granaries. And though it is unlikely that the prairie provinces with the exception of Manitoba will ever be able greatly to diversify their agriculture they are achieving a certain diversification through the growing importance of mining in their economy. In 1936 it had increased 22.8 per cent over 1935 and represented 8 per cent of the value of their net product. Since Manitoba has 16 per cent of Canada's available hydroelectric energy and Alberta and Saskatchewan together have 6 per cent, of which only 6.5 per cent has been developed; since three-fifths of the area of Manitoba is underlain by the Pre-Cambrian rocks which have been found so rich in minerals where explored in Northern Ontario and Quebec; since Alberta has splendid grazing lands in the foothills of the Rockies, the most extensive coal resources in Canada, and a major oilfield, there seems little reason to doubt that they will eventually be far less dependent on the state of the weather and the world wheat market than they are now.

Meanwhile the problem of keeping the western farmer going is far more difficult in Canada than in the United States. Canada's average wheat crop is 360,000,000 bushels and she consumes only a quarter of it herself. The American wheat crop is more than twice as great but the United States has twelve times as many people to eat it. The politically feasible device of bonusing crop restriction to bring agricultural prices in line with industrial ones may be, as its critics say, economically as efficient as burning the house down to make roast pig. But the United States can do it, since the domestic price is the important price for her farmers. The Canadian wheat-grower's ruling price is fixed for him in Liverpool. He is at the mercy of world forces. Efforts have been made for nearly ten years past to achieve a world wheat agreement but they have never succeeded. The European deficit countries have felt that they must protect their own peasants and achieve a maximum of self-sufficiency against the wrath to come. The Argentine did not wish to sacrifice the advantage it obtains from its ability and willingness to sell its wheat cheap.

There is another sort of farming to which Canada has been turning in increasing measure. That is fur farming. The story of the fur trade for a century and a half was the story of early Canada. The Canadian Indian had two things that were coveted by the first French colonizers, his soul and his furs. Sometimes his soul ran a bad second and was drowned in alcohol for the betterment of trade. So avid was New France for the red man's pelts that it neglected agriculture and industry to get them. After the English conquest it was the search for furs by the Hudson's Bay and the North West companies that opened up the West. In the early 1800's fur was still the most valuable export from Canada. Even today, though colonization has pushed wild life back, Northern Canada remains one of the world's chief sources of natural skins. The total output has not greatly diminished since the days when the Dominion was a wilderness, for the depletion of natural resources has been made good by fur farming. Whereas in 1921 the value of pelts of farm-bred animals was only 3 per cent of the raw fur production, in 1937 it was on the way to being 50 per cent. The silver fox, mink, raccoon, skunk, marten, fisher, and fitch have been civilized to the point where they thrive in complete captivity while the muskrat and the beaver have been persuaded to live and have their being in fenced areas of marsh and river. Fur farms now supply the bulk of silver fox pelts and the skin of the farm-bred mink is said to be better than that taken from the animal in his natural habitat.

Not only are the fur-bearers being raised domestically but they are being conserved in their wild state. Catches have been limited, closed seasons have been established, and game sanctuaries have been provided from which the country around may be restocked. Aided by the writings and lecturings of Gray Owl, a remarkable and somewhat mysterious figure who was variously described as Indian, halfbreed, and white man gone native, the beaver has been preserved when he seemed, at least in Eastern Canada, to be threatened with extinction. He is one of the emblems of Canada but for a time Canadians seemed determined to convert him into a purely heraldic animal.

Since Canada contains half the fresh water of the world and its coasts are washed by two oceans its fishing industry has long been important. Since fishing is better in the

colder northern waters American fishermen always wanted
to share the harvest of Canada's Atlantic coasts and in
earlier days disputes over this issue nearly led to war. But
now the Pacific salmon has become more important than
the Atlantic cod. Since 1895 it has been the most valuable
Canadian pack. Lobsters, which were once so plentiful in
Canada's Atlantic waters that after a storm the beach would
be littered with them, are in second place and cod third.
The value of Canada's fisheries, though it has declined
since the depression, is far greater now than it was when
fishing rights caused so much irritation with her southern
neighbor. The estimated value of the total catch in 1844
was only $125,000. In 1888, when the Chamberlain-Bayard
Fisheries Treaty at length settled the international fisheries dispute, it was valued at $20,000,000 and in 1918 at
$60,000,000. Since then prices have declined and the total
value of the catch with it. Inland fish represent only a fifth
of the total but their value in luring the American tourist
to Canada must be considerable. Like wheat-growing, fishing is largely an export industry in the Dominion, and the
United States, despite loud protests from Gloucester fishermen, takes half the exports.

14

Canada's Industry and Its Problems

THE outstanding features of Canada's economy, considered as a whole, are its dependence on a highly specialized export trade, its close affiliation with the United States, its high fixed costs, and its lack of diversification.

Canada exports 40 per cent of her net production or 21 per cent of her gross production as compared with 8 or 9 per cent for the United States. Seventy-eight per cent of her exports go to Great Britain and the United States. In 1937 Canada stood eighth among the countries of the world as an importer and fourth as an exporter. In 1929 she was fifth in both categories. Her share in world trade was 3.68 per cent in 1929 and 3.6 per cent in 1937. But in that time she had increased her share of exports by almost 10 per cent. She had done this in a world which was increasingly turning away from the old free interchange of goods toward bilateralism in trade and in some cases to straight barter; toward intra-imperialistic trade among those countries which formed part of imperial systems; toward the canalizing and arbitrary orientation of trade by means of exchange controls; toward autarchy and away from international specialization. The tendency of trade to become intra-imperialistic had been of benefit to her, since she·forms part of the greatest and wealthiest of the world's empires. All the other factors mentioned had militated against a country which as an exporter in huge quantities of a limited number of raw materials or semi-manufactured goods needed the freest possible access to all the world's markets.

Canadians are still living largely off the bounty of nature and spooning its abundance into the laps of highly industrialized countries like Great Britain and the United States. In the beginning she exported fur. Then it was softwood lumber. In 1890 came the railroad—and wheat. For sixteen years, with two exceptions, she was the world's greatest exporter of wheat. After the World War woodpulp and paper began to take the lead. The Canadian Shield furnished the trees and the waterpower. The newspapers of the United States, with their large circulations and their many pages, furnished the demand. The spruce, hemlock, balsam, and jackpine of Northern Ontario and Quebec replaced the vanishing forest resources of the United States as the American newsprint industry migrated north. Now the United States takes about 90 per cent of Canada's pulp and paper exports. In 1929 Canada exported as much newsprint as all other countries combined. But she is depleting her stands at such a rate that they may not last another forty-five years. Her pulp and paper manufacturers are mining her forests as some of her western farmers mined their land.

For the past decade the products of the mine have assumed increasing importance in Canada's production and exports. Whereas before 1924 she had been relatively un-

important as a mineral producer, in 1938 her mining and
metallurgical industries provided exports slightly greater
in value than those of either the fields or the forests of the
Dominion. Today few countries have better facilities for
the production of base metals, and rapid as has been its development it is obvious that what has been accomplished is
only a beginning. She owes this, like her pulp and paper
industry, to the Laurentian Shield, which, just as it provides waterpower and trees for the pulp and paper manufacturers, provides waterpower and ore for mining.

Canada now supplies 88 per cent of the world's nickel,
50 per cent of its asbestos, 12 per cent of its copper, 11 per
cent of its lead, 11 per cent of its zinc, 50 per cent of its
platinum. She is the fourth largest producer of gold and the
largest producer of radium. Wherever railroads have been
built through the Laurentian Shield, minerals have been
discovered. Now the airplane has supplemented the railroad as the prospector's aid. When gold was discovered at
Porcupine and Kirkland Lake the prospector was limited
to the distance a canoe would take him from the end of
steel. But in 1928 airplanes were setting down prospecting
parties not only in the remoter fastnesses of Ontario and
Quebec but as far north as Coronation Gulf and Victoria
Island in the Arctic. Air photography made possible the
rapid preparation of topographical maps and plotting of
geological data that would tell the prospector where to
look. Once claims are staked, diamond drills and light
machinery are flown in to facilitate their exploration. As
a result of all this, Canada's progress in mineral discovery
has been stepped up to a rate probably five times as great
as before the advent of the flying prospector, and mining

developments are pushing back the frontiers of settlement in a way reminiscent of the rush toward the western wheatlands in the 1900's.

There are two serious contradictions in this story of mineral development. Canada possesses 16 per cent of the world's coal reserves and her iron deposits are extensive and widely distributed. But she imports 50 per cent of the coal she consumes and since 1923 no iron ore has been mined in Canada. The trouble with coal is that it is in the wrong places and the trouble with iron is that it is too low-grade to compete with higher-grade iron from the United States. Eighty-seven per cent of Canada's coal is in Alberta. The rest is in British Columbia, even farther west, and in Nova Scotia, which is as far east as you can go in Canada. Ontario and Quebec, the two most thickly settled and highly industrialized Canadian provinces, are about 2000 miles away from Canada's western coal resources and almost 1000 miles away from the Nova Scotia mines. For twenty years the Dominion Steel and Coal Corporation has been exploiting Nova Scotian coal with the aid of iron ore from the easily accessible and high-grade Wabana deposits in near-by Newfoundland. But it goes down 3000 feet to get its coal and its shafts extend more than two miles under the sea. There is an iron and steel industry in Ontario which imports both its coal and iron, the former from the Pennsylvania fields and the latter from the Mesabi Range in Minnesota.

The unavailability of Canada's coal and iron resources was a serious, almost a fatal, handicap to her industrialization in the late nineteenth and early twentieth centuries, the age of steam and iron. But it is not so today. The malicious spirit which stole in to Canada's cradling and tossed the gifts her fairy godmother had left her into places where she could not easily use them could not have foreseen the age of electricity, of plastics and alloys, which is now dawning. For that age Canada is excellently equipped, because next door to one of the world's most important deposits of non-ferrous metals she has waterpower resources so extensive that although Canadians are the second largest users of hydroelectric power the energy available is only 19 per cent developed. Canada's waterpower is widely distributed, it is cheap to develop, and, most fortunately, Ontario and Quebec which have no coal, have most waterpower. The pulp and paper and the mining industries of the Canadian Shield use it extensively and 78 per cent of all Canadian manufacturing plants are now electrified. It so happens that just those non-ferrous metals, artificial abrasives, and chemicals such as fertilizers, acids, and sodium compounds which Canada produces in abundance can best use waterpower for their manufacture.

In the Turner Valley oilfield, some 45 miles southwest of Calgary, Alberta, Canada has what geologists believe may be one of the greatest oilfields in the world. It now produces almost 7,000,000 barrels annually of high-grade crude oil and some 90 billion cubic feet of natural gas, of which 78 billions is burned in the air for lack of a market. Seventy-five million dollars has been invested in the Turner Valley to date. At the outbreak of war the British Government, and particularly the British Admiralty, was inquiring into the potentialities of this important Empire field, and the construction of a 1500-mile pipeline eastward to the head of the Great Lakes has been discussed. It would cost $30,000,000 but might be justified both by the potentialities of the field as a commercial producer and by its strategic value to an Empire at war. Curiously enough, a German concern was interesting itself in such a project in 1938. When war broke out, the production of the Turner Valley field had been radically prorated but it has since been stepped up to meet the demands, especially for aviation gasoline, of the Canadian air scheme.

The trend of Canadian production is revealed by a comparison between 1926—considered a normal, pre-depression year—and 1938. In that twelve-year period the value of all Canadian field crops declined by more than 50 per cent; primary forest production by 20; pulp and paper products by 22; wood, wood products, and paper by 9; livestock and poultry by 21; dairy products by 33. But, although the production of pig iron dropped slightly and that of cement by 50 per cent, the output of all minerals increased 180 per cent. Gold production was up 270 per cent, copper 440 per cent, lead 145 per cent, zinc 250 per cent, nickel 320 per cent, crude petroleum 1900 per cent, asbestos 3.5 per cent. The output of central electrical stations had increased 35 per cent, installed horsepower 80 per cent, and net manufacturing production 7 per cent. The value of Canadian exports had declined to 80 per cent but their quantity had increased 7.3 per cent.

What this means is that the Canadian farmer and forester had not by 1938 recovered prices and markets but that the base metal industry had risen to swell the volume of production slightly above the pre-depression figure and to bring its value measurably close. There was not, however, a corresponding recovery of the national income.

An industry such as gold mining is highly important for a country's balance of payments with the outside world. But it does not give so much employment as does wheat farming, even the highly mechanized wheat farming of the Canadian West, nor does a dollar's worth of gold pass through so many Canadian hands. The whole non-ferrous metal products industry of Canada, the gross value of whose output is $351,000,000, pays only $45,000,000 a year in salaries and wages whereas the wood and paper products industry, although the value of its production is only 40 per cent more, has a wage and salary bill more than 300 per cent greater. There are no exact figures, but the disparity would be much greater if metal production and wheat farming were compared. If Canada manufactured all the mining machinery the non-ferrous metals industry requires, or converted its products into finished form, the effect of its prosperity on the national income would be far greater. The production of hydroelectric power, which has more than doubled since 1926, and in which more capital is invested than in any two of Canada's manufacturing industries combined, employs only 17,000 persons. But there is a saving circumstance. The production of electrical equipment, from huge generators to toasters, has become the ninth industry of Canada.

Ranking high as an employer of labor is the textile industry, which provides work for one out of every six Canadians engaged in manufacturing. Canada does not lack advantages for this type of production. Humidity and temperature control systems have to simulate the soft climate of Manchester and Huddersfield in her mills but they are situated on streams fed by mountain lakes which catch soft

rain water. Yet the textile industry is almost purely parasitic in Canada. Canadian silk stockings are said to be the
best in the world and are being increasingly exported.
Otherwise textile manufacture exists only by reason of the
tariff protection it enjoys. It has been estimated that of
forty leading Canadian industries at least twenty-four depend on tariffs wholly or partly for their existence. But the
automobile and rubber goods industries, which are also
exotic, have at least demonstrated their ability to export.
The textile industry has become notable only for its ability
to return imposing profits to its owners. In 1935 the Dominion Textile Company, which employs 41 per cent of
Canadian cotton workers, was shown by testimony before a
Royal Commission to have paid without interruption for
ten years dividends equal to 150 per cent on its original
investment and 22 per cent on a second stock subscription
in 1922. High tariffs have been justified in Canada as cre-
ators of employment. But the textile industry had slashed
wages by 10 and 20 per cent in 1933 and the highest wage
it was paying in 1935 was $15.71 a week. The Canadian
consumer did not seem to be getting off more lightly. The
NRA was able to restore the price of denim in the United
States in 1935 only to 14 cents per pound. But the Canadian price, without benefit of NRA, was 18¾ cents.

Canada has had tariff protection for its secondary industries since 1858. In 1879 a National Policy designed to foster them was adopted. The average ad valorem rate of duty
in the Canadian tariff ranged from 20 per cent in 1878 to
26 per cent in 1930 and 29 per cent in 1932. The Smoot-
Hawley tariff in the United States provoked in 1930 in
Canada the most drastic jacking up of duties since the Na-

tional Policy was adopted. During a Royal Commission inquiry into the relations between the Dominion and its province of Nova Scotia it was estimated by Professor Norman Rogers, now in Mr. Mackenzie King's cabinet, that in 1931 Canadians paid approximately $425,000,000 more than the world level of competitive prices to sustain their manufacturing institutions. Professor Rogers presented figures to prove that seven Canadian provinces were paying an annual toll of more than $80,000,000 to the protected industries of Ontario and Quebec. The cost of the tariff to the wheat-exporting prairie provinces was estimated at $55,000,000.

The Canadian people did not forgive Mr. R. B. Bennett for the 1931 tariff policy that created mushroom millionaires while the rest of Canada ate the bitter bread of the Great Depression. Mr. Bennett did not deserve all the reproaches that were heaped on him. For lack of other instruments he had tried to use the tariff as a means of providing unemployment relief, rectifying Canada's balance of payments, and controlling its exchange. He had exacted a promise from the heads of Canadian protected industry not to take advantage of higher duties to raise prices. They did not raise prices but, at a time when these were tumbling in the rest of the world, they maintained them. The Royal Commission which inquired in 1935 and 1936 into the results of these policies suggested that some relationship be established between the protection industries received and the profits they were allowed to extract from the general public. In the case of purely parasitic industries such as textile manufacturing, which plunder the farmer, miner, forester, and fisherman, there would seem to be an overwhelming argument for an arrangement of this kind. The only case that can be made out for them is that Canada needs population. Mining, though highly important as an export factor in Canada's economy, does not employ large numbers of men. Until Canada has more people to provide a home market for mass production the products of the mine will have to be exported only in a raw or semi-finished state. A parasitic industry such as textile manufacture, by preying on the non-ferrous metal industries, makes them indirectly support a larger population. It also, of course, increases their production costs. Apparently they can stand it but the western grain-grower, whose costs are also increased by the tariff, feels the burden. It has been equalized for him to some extent by minimum prices and crop bonuses. Against these handouts eastern mining, like other eastern manufacturing, has been protesting. It has found a mouthpiece in Premier Mitchell Hepburn of Ontario, who, though a farmer elected to office chiefly by the farm vote, is not the type of landowner who despises new wealth. Logically the up-and-coming mining industry should join itself with western agriculture in opposition to protective tariffs. But mining, like the exploitation of waterpower, requires large amounts of capital, and big business in Canada is all one happy family.

Though Canada is a young country her economy already reveals that hardening of the arteries of competition which exhibits itself in rigidity of structure and domination by finance capital. A parliamentary inquiry reported in 1935 a concentration of wealth which equaled that of the United States as recorded in the study by A. A. Berle and G. C. Means of 200 leading American companies. Of

Canada's 145 largest concerns 65 per cent, owning 77 per cent of all assets, were minority-controlled. Of these, nearly three-quarters fell into management-controlled or joint minority-management-controlled categories, where the management owned less than 20 per cent of the capital. Of 276 large Canadian companies 35.7 per cent were holding companies. There had been, it was found, a steady growth of large corporations in comparison with the general growth of business. There were in Canada 100 companies with assets of more than $10,000,000 each. There was a marked tendency toward large production units. In the United States manufacturing establishments with an output of $1,000,000 or more in 1929 represented 5.57 per cent of the number of plants but produced 69 per cent of total output. In Canada in 1929 plants with an output of more than $1,000,000 were 3.2 per cent of the total but produced 62 per cent of the total output.

It has been stated in the Canadian Parliament that a few hundred men, through interlocking directorates, control most of the business of Canada. One name that recurs 42 times in the board lists of important Canadian corporations is that of Sir Herbert Holt, chairman of the Royal Bank of Canada. The Royal Bank, the Bank of Montreal, and the Canadian Bank of Commerce own almost 70 per cent of all banking assets. Three-quarters of the tobacco smoked in Canada is made by the Imperial Tobacco Company and two-thirds of the oil and gasoline which Canadians consume is sold by the Imperial Oil Company. The Imperial Oil Company started as a Canadian concern in a small way but was adopted into the Standard Oil family in 1896. It sets prices not only for the consumer but for the three other, smaller companies with whose perfect concurrence it monopolizes the Canadian market. Having decided beforehand what portion of the consumer's dollar is to go for gasoline, they compete merely to see which gets the most of that generous allotment. So happily has this arrangement worked that the original $100 par common stock of Imperial Oil is now worth $2560 a share and pays a 160 per cent dividend to those lucky enough to have held it originally. The profits of the other three companies of the "Big Four," if not quite so fantastic, are fantastic enough for industries so heavily protected by a tariff.

Two classes of industry are dependent on the tariff in Canada, exotic industries of native origin such as textile and iron and steel manufacture, and Canadian branches of American industries. In nothing is Canada more American than in her financial and industrial relations. She is always either the first or second best customer of the United States, her annual imports sometimes approaching $1,000,000,000. She is the largest exporter to the American market. The United States has $4,000,000,000 invested in Canada, three times as much as in any other single country. American tourists spend twice as much there as they spend anywhere else. One fourth of all the manufacturing in Canada is done by American-controlled companies. They make 82 per cent of trucks and automobiles; 68 per cent of electrical apparatus; 50 per cent of non-ferrous metals; 44 per cent of non-metallic mineral manufactures; 42 per cent of agricultural, industrial, office, and household machinery; 41 per cent of chemicals; and 40 per cent of miscellaneous manufactures. In 1932 there were some 1200

American-controlled or -affiliated firms in Canada with a total capitalization of $2,167,249,000. Of these, 690 firms with a capitalization of $545,692,000 were employed in manufacturing; 115, capitalized at $287,600,000, made pulp and paper; 49 firms, capitalized at $236,599,000, were engaged in mining and smelting; 81 firms, capitalized at $707,751,000, were public utilities; 39 firms, capitalized at $97,882, were classed as "miscellaneous"; and 257, capitalized at $291,725,000, were occupied in selling.

The causes for this substantial direct United States investment in Canada are various. The fact that some 45 per cent of the newsprint produced in Canada is produced under American auspices is due to the exhaustion of United States pulpwood forests. Imperial preferences played a large part in bringing the American automobile industry across the border, since it can benefit under them when shipping from Canadian plants. Cheap hydroelectric power attracted such industries as aluminum manufacture, and power plus a bountiful supply of raw material was responsible for American participation in other branches of the non-ferrous metals industry. In some cases the inducement was profit. But in the great majority the tariff was the principal cause. American-controlled pulp and paper companies serve the United States alone. Most other branch plants find an Empire as well as a Canadian market. On the average 85 per cent of the product of American branch factories is actually produced in Canada but more than 75 per cent of the profits realized are remitted to the United States.

Canada, which is so British in many things, is not British in the matter of branch plants. There were only 98 manufacturing concerns in Canada in 1932 owned or controlled by Great Britain and the capital they employed was only 20 per cent of the American total. In the past few years, however, probably because of the threat of war, an increasing interest has been shown by British industry in the Canadian field.

Anxiety lest this American economic penetration might lead to political control has not seemed to worry Canadians. They have discouraged American investment in banks, airways, and the radio but otherwise let it take its course. There is actually only a slight American financial interest in Canadian railroads, trucking companies, telegraphs, cables, and wireless, and electrical power production and distribution are 80 per cent Canadian-controlled. All told, about 62 per cent of Canada's business capital is Canadian. The only political influence American branch plants have ever tried to exert in Canada has been to maintain the tariff that gave them birth. The New York money market is believed to have made its views quietly known from time to time on some aspects of Canadian financing but there has never been any open example of pressure by American investors on the Canadian Government such as was exercised by the English shareholders of the Grand Trunk Railway, who rejected the Government's offer for that bankrupt road and were awarded much less by a board of arbitration.

Canadians can also urge, as was pointed out by Herbert Marshall and Frank Southard, Jr., in their study of Canadian-American industry for the Carnegie Endowment for International Peace, that "relative to wealth and population, Canadians have as large industrial invest-

ments in the United States as Americans have in Canada."
Canadian-owned companies in the United States number
about 170, aside from American branches of Canadian
banks and insurance companies and the New York offices
of investment bankers.

American and British capitalists have combined to
finance some of Canada's most important individual companies. The gigantic du Pont explosive and chemical interests in the United States are linked with the great Imperial Chemical Industries company of Great Britain by
Canadian Industries, Limited, which dominates Canadian
chemical production, but is only 10 per cent Canadian-
owned. Its president, Mr. A. B. Purvis, has taken the wartime job of directing all Allied buying in the United
States. Forty-two per cent of the shares in the International Nickel Company are owned by Americans and 33
per cent by British capitalists. It possesses more than 90 per
cent of the world's nickel deposits and was attacked, during the World War and before this one, for letting nickel
reach German armament makers. Lord Robert Cecil complained in 1916 that nickel had been shipped from the
United States in the submarine *Deutschland*. But Sir
Robert Borden, Canada's wartime Prime Minister, opposed prohibition of export because, among other reasons,
"it would create strained relations with the United States
and might provoke retaliation." He pointed out that
Major Graham Bell, one of the ablest officers in the British
civil service, had been detailed to prevent supplies of this
armament essential from getting to Germany. France,
whose island of New Caledonia contains most of the 12
per cent of the world's nickel not produced in Canada,

prohibited its export to foreign countries in 1934. An embargo on its export from Canada to Germany has been urged in the British and Canadian Parliaments but officially disapproved. The reasons in favor of it have seemed strong.

The International Nickel Company has been stronger. British and American newspapermen including the writer, who visited the company's Frood mine in 1939 to see King George and Queen Elizabeth descend into its depths in the course of the royal tour, received a distinct impression of extraterritoriality once they entered its high gates. Ferocious mosquitoes bit them and hard-faced "company cops" looked as if they would like to. They were firmly refused permission to share the perils and secrets of the mine with Their Majesties. Mr. Mackenzie King, ever courteous, asked that the ban be lifted. But Canada's Prime Minister was also refused—politely. Actually one English newspaperman, who arrived late with the royal party, by an oversight was allowed like it to don canvas canonicals and profane the subterranean temple. Since he learned no secrets the company's action must have been merely the expression of an attitude—that attitude toward the public so aptly expressed through another newspaperman by William H. Vanderbilt of the New York Central.

Most of Canada's big businessmen are Scotch Canadians. Despite the importance of American capital in Canada, the newspapers they control profess an ardent imperialism and they themselves are as a class fiercely, and it could be said blindly, pro-British. They do not seem to feel the same loyalty to Canada. Some of the wealthiest of them, grumbling at Canadian taxation, have retired to the West

Indies while others have found a home and a title in Great
Britain, where the present rate of taxation is almost con-
fiscatory. Their attitude seems to be a resultant of the
Canadian Loyalist tradition combined with the Ulster
Loyalist tradition and accentuated perhaps by an uncon-
scious feeling that as they have a lien on the body of
Canada its soul might well be treated as a colonial com-
modity to be delivered F.O.B. in the British market. But as
businessmen, if more conservative and less enterprising
than their American equivalents, they have been equally
as efficient and more *suaviter in modo* if *fortiter in re*.

15

Canada's Finances and Their Future

CANADA'S industrial system, except that it is far less self-contained, closely resembles that of the United States. Her banking system is different. The United States has what might be described as a democratic banking system. Canada's is hierarchical and far sounder. The government-owned Bank of Canada regulates credit, acts as fiscal agent for the Dominion Government, manages the public debt, and controls exchange. It is taking over from the chartered commercial banks their note issues.

The commercial banks are all organized on the branch system. Some American states claim to have had unhappy experience with branch banks but they have been of great value to Canada. Because of them her banking system is more centralized and more flexible than that of the United States. They have assisted the growth of the Canadian West by enabling eastern savings to be lent to the prairie farmers by western branches. In 1913 one bank's loans in the West were five times as great as the savings deposits which originated there. Farmers have complained that rates were too high, loans for too short a term, and that the system made for monopoly and eastern domination.

The Canadian system showed its value in the depression, when no banks failed, although many a Canadian industry complained that they had stepped dryshod to safety only by pushing it under. The last bad failure in Canada was that of the Home Bank in 1923. But there have been many absorptions so that now, aside from government and other savings institutions, only 10 banks remain, and of these three are more important than all the rest. Even before the advent of the Bank of Canada the Canadian Bankers' Association, a body whose equivalent does not exist in the United States, facilitated the co-operation of the individual banks and tended to link their credit and policies.

It is well that Canadian banks have been conservative, since Canadians themselves, like Americans fifty years ago, tended to put two parts of native optimism together with two parts of borrowed money and trust to the future to make it five. Canada borrowed from London the money to finance the colonization of the West. In 1914 Britain had $2,700,000,000 invested in Canada, slightly more than she has today. American investment was less than $1,000,000,000. Canadians had not thought of themselves as investors or were perhaps too busy spending money to think of saving it. But during the war the Canadian Government was astonished to discover that it could borrow $2,000,000,000 from its own people. British investing stopped but the United States stepped obligingly into the breach and increased her investment to some two billion dollars.

The war increased Canada's federal national debt from $500,000,000 to $2,700,000,000. But it left her with a credit balance of $600,000,000 on a total trade worth $2,500,-000,000. Her dollar was at a discount and she was unable to return to the gold standard until 1926. But Europe needed the products of Canada's war-stimulated industries for rehabilitation and for a time the produce of her war-enlarged agriculture. This trade, together with larger United States investment and a growing American tourist traffic, tided her over what might otherwise have been a difficult period. But she was increasing her public indebtedness. In 1929 it had reached $5,000,000,000. Instead of paying it off with the surplus of payments which she had accumulated she used this to buy foreign securities on her own account.

As a result, when the slump came in 1930, Canadians had become per capita the third largest foreign investors in the whole world. Canada's foreign indebtedness was greater than that of any other country except Germany. The two facts did not turn out to be compensatory, since a substantial portion of Canada's foreign claims was frozen by the depression, while she had to make good in American dollars the bonds on which she rashly had guaranteed optional payment. This became a grievous burden when she had to follow Britain off the gold standard and let her dollar sink to a 15 per cent discount. But she tightened her belt with the help of the Bennett tariff and met her liabilities so well that the Foreign Bondholders Protective Council—which reported in 1935 that 40 per cent of European government bonds and 82 per cent of Latin-American bonds held by American investors were in default—announced that only .8 per cent of Canadian public bonds had been repudiated.

Finally the United States went off the gold standard. It was a lifesaver for Canada, since it abolished the premium of her debts and increased the price of her exports. When she again had her head above water she found that the United States Security Act of 1933 had made it difficult for her to resume borrowing, even to refund former loans at lower rates. As a result few Canadian loans have been floated in the American market since 1933 and what refunding operations have been carried out have been largely the result of private banking arrangements in New York. A few federal and provincial loans were floated in England.

During the ten years from 1929 to 1938 Canada had on balance exported almost half a billion dollars of capital and reduced her indebtedness abroad by almost a billion. Her net debt on entering the present war was $3,101,-000,000, about twice as great as in 1919. Before the World War the Dominion had a surplus of imports, like any other young country which is borrowing heavily to expand. Since the World War, with interruptions, she has had a surplus of exports. This means that she has now become a mature debtor country. Instead of contracting new foreign debts she is paying off old ones. She will pay off more of them, willy nilly, as a result of this war, since Britain, to finance her war purchases in Canada, must repatriate the Canadian securities she holds, and Canada under American neutrality regulations cannot raise new loans in the United States. Britain has $1,000,000,000 invested in Canadian railways; $500,000,000 in the securities of Canadian governments; $377,000,000 in manufacturing industries; $185,000,000 in public utilities; $161,-

000,000 in financial and mortgage companies; $89,000,000 in mining companies; $87,000,000 in insurance concerns; $74,000,000 in merchandising and service companies.

Fifty-two per cent of the common and 97 per cent of the preferred shares of the Canadian Pacific Railway are held in England. Of Canada's two transcontinental railroads one, the Canadian National, is already government-owned. If Britain repatriates her C.P.R. shares, the Canadian Government, unless it resells them to its public or to Americans, will own both of Canada's two great transportation systems. Mr. King's American-born Minister of Transport, Mr. C. D. Howe, told the writer he thought the Government would prefer to have the C.P.R. privately owned and thus a yardstick for the nationalized C.N.R.

The railroad problem is a burning one in Canada, far more so even than in the United States. More than half the public debt of the Dominion was incurred in the construction or bonusing of railways. She made two great mistakes: she built three transcontinental roads, which was one too many; her government guaranteed the stock of one of them, now part of the Canadian National. As a result she has more miles of railroad per capita than any other country in the world and only three other countries have more absolute mileage. Her investment in railroads is $400 per capita and the annual deficit on the Canadian National Railways costs every Canadian $4.50 a year. Her freight rates are among the lowest in the world. In other words, Canada taxes herself to maintain her west to east axis, to foster her national unity, and to bonus her western farmers.

For the past ten years Sir Edward Beatty, president of

the privately owned C.P.R., has been urging with the
support of Eastern chambers of commerce that "the railway problem" be solved. Amalgamation of the two roads,
preferably under C.P.R. auspices, it has been represented,
would more than meet the annual deficit on the C.N.R.
Voluntary "co-operation" of the two roads as recommended
by a royal commission has effected economies much smaller
than that. The Government apparently does not believe
that amalgamation would save much more. The Canadian
West accuses Sir Edward of being more concerned for the
fortunes of his British shareholders than for the Canadian
exchequer. The dispute has often been represented as being between efficient private enterprise and wasteful public ownership. But actually the Canadian Government
owns the C.N.R. only because it came to the rescue of de-
funct private enterprise. It partly built and heavily endowed the C.P.R. The issue is of more than general
interest to the United States, for Americans are heavy
holders of Canadian National stock.

Since almost 80 per cent of Canada's exports go to Britain and the United States, Canada's future is bound up
not only with their prosperity but with their tariff policies.
She need not worry about access to the British market
while the war endures. The Ottawa agreements of 1932
bound the Empire together. The trade control measures
adopted since the war began have tightened these links
into the closest integration achieved since early colonial
times. Great Britain has bought up many of the export
staples of the Empire for the duration or guaranteed their
prices. Nearly all her colonies and most of the dominions
have applied import controls against non-Empire goods.

Canada has done this also but as against the United States has been more concerned to control the character of her imports than to restrict their volume.

In normal times the American market is the only one really adequate to Canada's needs. She has never had more than a part of it. She could probably sell 60,000,000 bushels of hard wheat annually in the United States but the American farmer has seen to it that she did not get a chance and Canada has retaliated by shutting out the American manufacturer. Despite this Canada and the United States do the greatest two-country trade in the world. It is often said that their resources are too alike to form a basis for commerce. This is one of those generalizations which when examined in detail lose most of their validity. There is an obvious basis for the exchange of Canadian forest products, fish, nickel, and asbestos against American cotton, semi-tropical fruits, tobacco, and petroleum.

There are other resources which are complementary rather than competitive. Many vegetables and fruits ripen early in the United States and late in Canada. Under an intelligent tariff policy they would move north at one season, south at another. Since the boundary between the two countries is almost 4000 miles long and their populations are spread out along it, since Canada has coal deposits in the West and the United States in the East, transportation costs would often be far lower across the boundary then parallel to it. A great deal of frontier trade could be carried on with advantage to both countries.

In the industrial field Canada has waterpower and nonferrous metals complementary to the coal, oil, and iron of the United States. It is uneconomical for Canada to make iron and steel under present conditions but no country in the world is better equipped to manufacture the electric alloy steels and non-ferrous alloys that modern industry increasingly needs. The economy of this continent would be greatly improved if United States tariffs were altered to permit imports of industrial raw materials and the semi-manufactured products of Canadian metal and power resources, and Canadian tariffs were lowered on finished products made from these materials. Already there are metallurgical, chemical, and pulp and paper companies that use Canadian power and send their products to the United States for finishing.

What is to be Canada's economic future? She labors under certain distinct handicaps. A parliamentary inquiry on "price spreads" in 1935 pointed out the increasing inflexibility of her economy. While the prices of agricultural commodities vary in response to world and even domestic conditions, those of manufactured goods, sheltered behind a tariff or restricted by patents and cartels, are relatively rigid. Large areas are suitable only for growing wheat. Other regions have only mineral and pulp resources and development must proceed along those lines or not at all. The Canadian climate makes necessary in the way of railways, harbor facilities, and canals a great capital equipment capable of carrying a peak load within a short season but partly or completely idle for a considerable part of the year. The very size of Canada makes necessary an expensive transportation system and her winter climate heightens the cost of raising livestock, manufacturing goods, and keeping her communications open. With a varying income from exports and rigid costs she is unhappily situated when rapid economic readjustments must be made. Her public debt was 47 per cent more per capita than that of the United States when the war broke out and her income tax was higher.

Because of all these things many have set narrow limits to Canada's future. One of the most pontifical of American business magazines not long ago concluded that she could probably never support more than 18 to 25 million people. Her exports, it was declared, rested on a precarious base. Her recent boom in metals was accounted for by $35 gold and European rearmaments. Her newsprint production varied with United States advertising volume. Her wheat crop depended on the weather,

These objections are not impressive. It is true that Canada's agriculture and extractive industries are hitched to world markets today but so were American agriculture, the American lumber industry, and the American mining industry a half-century ago. All agriculture depends upon the weather and Canada's wheat farmers have sometimes made more money from a short crop than a bountiful one. If United States advertising volume falls off, more than the Canadian newsprint industry is bound to suffer. The United States, with her present huge stock of the metal, has a bigger stake in gold than Canada has. If Canada's prosperity depends largely upon that of Great Britain and the United States so does the prosperity of the rest of the world. If Canadian foreign trade hinges on the export of a comparatively few specialties most of them are materials that the world cannot long do without. Canada in any case is beginning to semi-manufacture her exports. Seventy

years ago she sent her wood abroad in the form of logs.
Today less than 10 per cent is so exported. Wheat flour,
cereal foods, dairy products, dressed meats, lumber, shin-
gles, pulp and paper, refined metals, cured and canned
fish, farm implements, automobiles, rubber goods, electrical apparatus, and whisky are manufactured or semi-
manufactured commodities that form an increasing share
of Canada's foreign shipments.

And Canada has one advantage that is seldom taken
into the calculations of those who measure her economy.
She is excellently situated to prosper in wartime, and since
Europe and Asia have been intermittently at war for the
past five years and seem likely to be steadily engaged in
martial activities for at least the next three, that is a substantial consideration. Aside from the United Kingdom
less than 7 per cent of her exports go to Europe. The rest
goes to North and South America, Asia, Africa, and
Oceania. Her trade, therefore, instead of being interrupted is likely to be stimulated by a European war.

The World War increased her exports of forest products from $43,000,000 in 1914 to $148,000,000 in 1918;
manufactured exports from $67,600,000 to $519,600,000;
minerals, $59,200,000 to $145,000,000. By 1918 the Imperial Munitions Board was spending $1,000,000 a day in
Canada for shells, propellants, explosives, acetone, TNT,
aluminum, nickel, airplane parts, agricultural machinery,
timber, and railway material. Her steel production increased from 800,000 to 2,250,000 tons annually, her industrial establishments from 21,000 to 38,000, her industrial output from $1,407,000,000 to $3,520,000,000. This
war, if it lasts long enough, can hardly do less, since Brit-

ain without American loans must buy more in Canada and less in the United States. It is true that it will probably leave Canada with a staggering load of debt but it will be, because it must be, an internal debt.

The record shows that Canada, without any New Deal of her own if a substantial indirect benefit from Mr. Roosevelt's pump priming, recovered from the 1930 depression more quickly than the United States. She benefited from the 1937 boomlet in the United States and did not react so decidedly in 1938. In 1937 her corporations showed a record rate of profit. Since the present war began, all her indices of production again point upward.

If the war resulted only in the establishment in Canada of the British equivalent of her 1200 American branch plants it would bring her economy substantial benefit. If it involved a substantial transference of British industry and population to the Dominion it would automatically solve the majority of her most pressing present problems. Given another 5,000,000 people, many of her tariff-fostered industries could reduce production and distribution costs to a point where they would cease to be parasitic. An increased home market will never solve the difficulties in this century of the prairie grain-grower, since to absorb his present export surplus Canada would require a population of at least 60,000,000. But it would make a permanently paying enterprise of eastern agriculture and it would allow the diversification of industry to proceed.

Although Canada has so much room her economy, as will be apparent from what has gone before, is not of the type which attracts large numbers of settlers and quickly absorbs them. She has no longer available large areas of soil adaptable to mixed farming on which new settlers can quickly make themselves self-sufficient. Her western wheatlands are suitable only for a large-scale, highly mechanized type of farming. Her extractive industries require large amounts of capital but not of men. In her industry and commerce monopoly abounds and wealth is concentrated. Her economy presents the picture of a vast land through which stalk a few saurian figures, a huge herbivorous dinosaur known as agriculture, smaller creatures which live off fish and wood, and carnivorous monsters which prey on them when they are not mating or warring with each other. Canada is austere rather than ample, more demanding than gracious, to be subjugated rather than wooed. She is being exploited increasingly by money and machinery rather than by men. Unless there is a wartime transplantation of British population she will be unable to obtain many new settlers except by planning a place for them in her economy. This would require a radical change from her recent policy. When the Bata Shoe Company of Czechoslovakia planned to build a factory in Canada and import Czech technicians the Canadian Government, after the example of the United States Department of Labor, insisted that only a few key men be admitted. It was reported that similar difficulties had arisen over the importation of technicians to establish glass and china industries.

The fact that Canada is not attracting a larger population does not mean that she could not support one. She has food and waterpower and wood and minerals enough for 60,000,000 people and she has so much capital that for the past fifteen years she has been investing it abroad rather than at home. It is true that she could never be self-sufficient and will prosper best in a world where trade is free. This economic fact contrasts harshly with the political course of her present rulers, which has tended steadily toward isolationism.

It has been urged that in a world heading for autarchy Canada's future is black. But if Britain and France win this war autarchy will have short shrift, for that is one of the things they are fighting against. It has been said that Canada is in a precarious position because she is dependent on world markets. But those nations which, like the United States, are almost completely self-sufficient and can make themselves independent of world markets, have not demonstrated that this allows them to solve their economic problems. Canada will have a difficult task of reconstruction after this war as after the last one. But she has been warned by experience, and her government, in all that it does now, is considering what it must do then. Her people have a stern climate to discipline them and rich resources to exploit. Though behind them lies a long history of pioneering, before them a receding frontier still beckons to the beyond. Theirs is a northern fate but not unkind, for the pot of gold with which they bought their way out of the last depression was found at the end of the aurora borealis. Their future problems may be hard but they can be trusted to solve them, for they have solved harder ones in the past.

16

Recapitulation

THE attempt has been made, in foregoing chapters, to describe Canada, to estimate her vast potentialities, to measure her not inconsiderable development of them, and to indicate the highly complicated character of her population, her politics and economics. It has been claimed for her that she is of great importance in her own right and of even greater importance as the last substantial link between the Western Hemisphere and the Eastern, between the British and American branches of the English-speaking people, between the New World democracies and the Old. It has been explained how—with her loyalties pulling her in one direction, her interests in another—she is a problem, not only for the United States and Great Britain, but for herself.

Canada's government has been criticized for trying to escape that problem in peacetime by abstaining from Empire affairs and for not seeking to control them in her own interests. It was pointed out that her policy of "no consultation for fear of commitment" since the last war has not prevented her commitment to participation in the present one, but has allowed her to blunder with Britain into a struggle rendered still more desperate by the fact that the United States has this time stood aloof. Whatever the out-

come of the war, Canada, it was admitted, would be protected by the Monroe Doctrine from German aggression.
But she would not be saved from heartbreak, since this
country, which began as an organized protest against the
American Revolution, was still ineradicably British.

Canada's recent history was reviewed to show how
Mackenzie King had, unnoticed except by constitutional
lawyers, taken a long step toward independence in the very
act of declaring war. He had had King George declare war
on the advice of his Canadian ministers for the first time
in Empire history, thus asserting Canada's right to elect for
neutrality if she chose and converting the Anglo-Canadian
tie into a personal union.

He had maneuvered not only his own following but his
Conservative opponents into a pledge against conscription,
and his tactics seemed likely to ensure that this would be
the last time Canada fought in Europe. Meanwhile he
seemed to be pursuing a policy of limited participation,
designed to keep Canada strong, united, and passive,
whether to make her the chief unit in the Empire after an
exhausting war, or to prepare her for independence, only
time could show.

Reasons were given why Canada, although older and
larger than the United States, was a failure so far as population was concerned. It was emphasized that Canada's
English-speaking population was still so British that disloyalty in Canada meant not disloyalty to Canada but only to
Britain. Her loyalty had cost her dear, but the last war had
left her a nation. This war might leave her the center of
the British Empire, if the United States were willing, or
convert her into a British refuge if Germany won. To the

latter course, it was predicted, Americans would make no objection, the less so since, if Germany won, the United States would need all the resources that might be salvaged in Canada from the wreck of the British Empire to help her defend the Western Hemisphere against certain attack. The opinion was expressed that, unless it were to rescue the Allies from certain and overwhelming defeat if the war should take that course, and perhaps not even then, the United States would continue to stand on the sidelines.

Much has happened since this book was undertaken and much is happening while these final words are being written. Nothing that has yet happened has shaken the views already set forth. Many things have confirmed them. The war has suddenly ceased to be that "competition in boredom" of which Lord Halifax spoke. Totalitarian war is swiftly assuming the aspect of total war. The world has already been made unsafe for neutrals, a dire fact of which even the biggest and strongest of them all, the United States, has suddenly been made aware. The narrow front behind which, it had been freely predicted, two rival armies of equal strength might crouch in a perpetual stalemate, has overnight been extended to more than twice its length. It has quickly been made apparent that in this war, as in the last, men and not merely machinery will be needed to fight it to a conclusion.

The invasion of Scandinavia made Greenland, as well as Canada, a potential issue with Germany under the Monroe Doctrine. Denmark sold the Virgin Islands to the United States during the last war because she was informed that if she fell under the domination of another European power the United States might have to take them without paying for them. In return Denmark asked, and apparently obtained, an assurance that no objection would be made to extension of her occupation of Greenland.

And then the dreaded thing happened. Overnight she was engulfed by the brown flood, and the ownership of another and larger Danish possession in the Western Hemisphere came in question under the Monroe Doctrine. The Faeroes, on the other hand, fell to Great Britain. When the news of their occupation reached Berlin, a German official spokesman was quoted by the Associated Press as commenting that "the real purpose is to have a mid-Atlantic base to facilitate the flight of the British Government to Canada."

Since this book was undertaken, too, an American minister to Canada evened the scales against Colonel Lindbergh, who had thought Canada should not be allowed to endanger the neutrality of the United States, by publicly expressing the opinion that the United States should intervene with Canada on the side of the Allies. Attorney-General Gordon Conant of Ontario blurted out on the public platform that "it is Canada's duty to do everything within our power to enlist the active support of the United States in the cause of the Allies." His speech was deeply resented by American isolationists. But they should have been grateful, for surely never had propaganda appeared in a form so open and undisguised—and so ineffective.

What Mr. Conant said would have been clearest common sense if he had said it in private to his own colleagues, or if he had said it in public before the war began. It would have been statesmanship of a high order if he had

not only said it before the war began but added "and to see
that the Allies do not alienate the active sympathies of the
United States."

But Mr. Conant might plead that the suggested addition
to his remarks would not then have been well received in
Toronto, where he presides over the legal activities of
Premier Mitchell Hepburn's government.

In a chapter on French Canada, the view was expressed
that French Canadians might find a better solution of their
racial problem in a polyglot British Empire in whose destinies Canada played a major part than in Canada as a
satellite of the United States. Pertinent to this contention
are the accumulating evidences, noted in April by a London correspondent of the New York *Times,* that Britain
and France are engaged in an effort for permanent, not
merely wartime, federation; that the present British Government is "launched upon a serious campaign to make
England and France not only one nation now, not only one
nation in a peace conference, but one nation so far as other
nations are concerned, forever." The correspondent went
on to ask: "What about the dominions when the Mother
Country brings this new member of the family into the
home?"

As far as the Dominion of Canada is concerned, such a
federation might settle her chief domestic problem. If
France and Britain could live peacefully under one constitutional roof, there would be no reason for English and
French Canadians to do otherwise. There would be no
excuse for English Canadians to refuse to learn French or
French Canadians to refuse to learn English. Canada's importance in the British Empire, as a dominion racially pat-

terned after the parent federation, would be greater than ever. Still greater would become her fitness for the role of interpreter between America and Europe. It would be strange to see the consequences of one war undone by another almost two centuries later and the Old World redressing the balance of the New.

For that to happen the Allies must win the war. If they lost it, other consequences would follow in the New World, not less interesting. Perhaps the most important would be that the United States would inevitably be driven into imperialism on a grand scale. As this is being written, plans are being discussed for her to spend still more billions for her own protection. If she had to face a Europe dominated by Germany, she would have to see that the other nations of the Western Hemisphere also financed and organized their defenses, now—with the exception of Canada's—totally inadequate.

South America would be the most vulnerable point of attack. No enemy could be allowed a real foothold in South America if North America were to be safe. For, if that happened, the United States would lose the advantage of the Atlantic and the Pacific Oceans that now separate her from her potential enemies. But a victorious Germany would enjoy tremendous prestige in Latin America and democracy little or none. If Germany maintained her alliance with Russia, she would have a double-headed appeal to the discontented elements in those none too stable republics south of the Equator. Rather than allow a puppet government to be set up anywhere in South America, the United States would have to become a strict rather than a good neighbor. She would have to coerce if the other weapons of imperialism failed. She would have to organize South America as Germany would organize Europe. She would have to do all those things, not because she wanted to, but because she must.

Where Britain had ruled only a quarter of the globe, the United States must dominate half.

No doubt it could be done, but would it be isolation?

INDEX

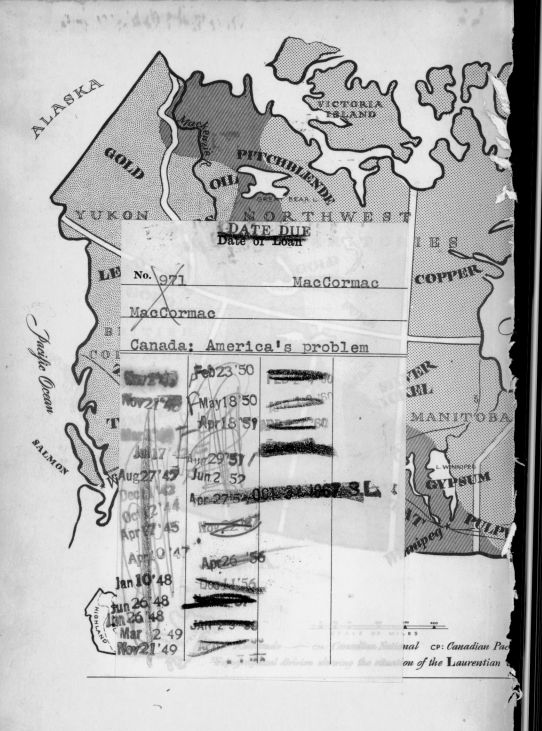